W9-AZS-632

EDITORS' CHOICE

Wisconsin's Best Hunting & Fishing Locations

By The Editors of

Published by:

**krause
publications**

700 E. State Street • Iola, WI 54990-0001

Please call or write for our free catalog of outdoor publications.
Our Toll-free number to place an order or obtain a free catalog is
800-258-0929. Please use our regular business telephone number
715-445-2214 for editorial comment or further information.

Library of Congress Catalog Number: 94-61205

ISBN: 0-87341-394-6

Printed in the United States of America

Contents

Introduction

Wisconsin's Best Hunting & Fishing Destinations

Where are the ten best fishing locations in Wisconsin? And what about the ten best hunting locations?

When I posed that question to the editors of *Wisconsin Outdoor Journal,* I knew they would list some outstanding destinations. After all, keeping tabs on what's going on in Wisconsin's outdoor world is their job, something they do better than anyone else. But how could they narrow the choices to the ten best in a state as blessed with natural resources as Wisconsin?

I was impressed with their efforts, and I believe they accomplished the goal that was given them. Read Tom Muench's report on the Black River and tell me you don't want to cast a line there. I bet you can't. Tell me that you can't read Dave Otto's chapter on the Navarino Wildlife Area without wanting to lace up your boots, uncase your favorite shotgun, and follow your dog for a few miles on a crisp October day.

There are some notable destinations that were left out, like musky fishing on Pewaukee or North Twin lakes or smallmouth bass fishing on Chequamegon Bay. Or bear hunting in the Chequamegon National Forest or deer hunting in some remote, gaslight-lit shack in the Nicolet National Forest, where the full moon illuminates a buck hanging from the meatpole and venison tenderloins are sizzling in a griddle atop a woodstove. If you are wondering why those places are not included in this book, just think of how special the twenty included here are.

Read about Wisconsin's best hunting and fishing destinations and plan to visit them someday. You won't be disappointed.

Steve Heiting
Editor
Wisconsin Outdoor Journal

Chapter 1

Drifting The 'Nammy

by Dave Carlson
Northwest Field Editor

Perfect candy-cane-shaped whoosh ... whoosh casts deliver a dry fly to flat water beneath a wood-pier bridge.

Downstream, musky baits arc in early morning mist to an eddy behind a log protruding from shore. A few miles away, a walleye worm rig carries monofilament line into a deep, dark pool. Around a few bends, a smallmouth tail dances across a rapids, spitting the floating bait briefly linking it with an angler.

Amidst this angling action, canoe paddles dip into the current or glance off rocks.

Picnic baskets and blankets unfold. Cameras click at eagles, mink, blue herons or fleeing bear and deer.

Hikers' feet shuffle along a streamside trail. Tent stakes are driven into loamy earth. Fish fry in an iron skillet over an open campfire.

All of it a mosaic of the burgeoning recreational scene offered by the northwest Wisconsin's still-wild Namekagon River.

Native Americans and non-Indian explorer-trappers traveling the Namekagon's 98-mile course (Namekagon Lake near Cable to a confluence with

Photo courtesy Dave Carlson

Northwest Field Editor Dave Carlson works on a shorelunch prior to a morning of fishing.

the St. Croix River north of Highway 77) would find a changed Namekagon, but in more ways than many rivers, very much as it was centuries ago.

Gone are virgin blocks of white pine and hemlock. The city of Hayward — a bustling tourist center — and a half-dozen or so logging-era hamlets, and many bridges straddle its banks. Some seasonal cabins and year-round residences dot the marsh-woodlands buffering the river from development. But the atmosphere is "wilderness." That thanks in part to the Namekagon's designation in 1972 as part of the National Wild and Scenic Riverway system. Most cases, in a matter of minutes after leaving landings, you become one with the "old" Namekagon — as thousands have discovered.

Divide the "Nammy," as anglers know it, this way: the upper portion is Class II trout cold-water, Hayward to Trego Flowage is cold water-warm water transitional, and below Trego Flowage is walleyes-muskies-smallmouth warmwater.

"The Namekagon's trout fishery is in excellent shape," says Frank Pratt, DNR Hayward-area fish manager. "And it is a pretty good warmwater fishery."

And, Pratt is quick to add: "Coldwater portions are moderately fished, warmwater are lightly fished."

Leon Pastika, a Hayward sports shop owner for four decades, rates flyfishing pressure "heavy at times."

"There's lots of catch and release going on," Pastika says, and while the river "might not be as good as 26 years ago, it's still very good."

Brown trout, rainbows and wild brook trout cruise the river upstream from Highway 63 to Pacawong Dam. Only artificials can be used in this eight-mile stretch, and a slat limit protects 10-inch to 16-inch

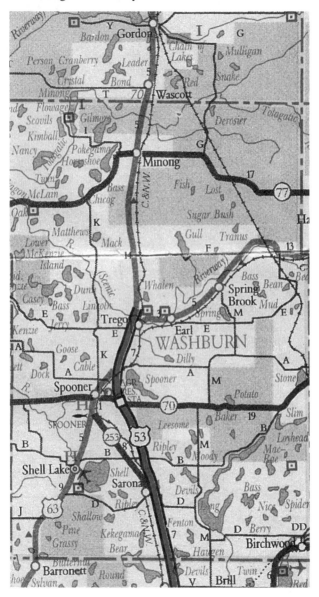

trout. From Phipps to Airport Road the limit is three trout.

Pratt's surveys reveal angling pressure of 300-plus trips per mile annually in this section. A 1987 fish survey, to be updated by the summer of 1994, revealed 30 to 35 16-inch or LARGER trout per mile! After a preliminary analysis of the new data, Pratt says: "We see even more big fish than 1987. We have some gaps (due to drought and harsh winters impacting production) but we have a lot of smaller fish coming in, too. It's very productive. We've got every insect known in the Midwest. I would rank this portion of the Namekagon with any of Upper Midwest's big fish fisheries."

Trout fishing downstream from the Lake Hayward Dam is unique in Wisconsin: a nine-inch, three trout daily limit during the regular inland trout ending Sept. 30, and catch and release with artificials-only angling Oct. 1 until the next year's general opening. Tailwaters below the Hayward Dam host browns (up to 22 inches), rainbows (16-inch varieties) and brook trout (up to 18 inches!) "The brookies are wild fish out of unnamed, unlisted streams and they're over-wintering in the Namekagon, and by early May they're gone," Pratt says. "Catch rate in this section are not extraordinary, about one trout for every three hours fishing. We've got giant stoneflies (size 4) hatching in March and April, and real tiny midges (18-20). You can see people flyfishing on warm February days. There's nothing like it in Wisconsin."

Moving downstream, there are fewer and fewer trout, and more and more smallmouth bass, walleyes and muskies in a warmwater environment lined with steep sandy banks, wide marshes, and pine and oak ridges and sprinkled with aspen and tag alder. It's here you'll most likely hear laughter of innertubers, kayakers or conoeists gliding moderately challenging whitewater riffles and deceptively fast flatwater.

Bob Kinderman, owner of Quiet Sports Outfitters at Trego, rents and shuttles canoes, kayaks and camping gear for Namekagon excursions. "Ten years ago there was practically nothing compared to today," Kinderman says. "You get a nice Memorial Day or weekend, and you're going to have traffic. But there are lots of bends and with the river flowing pretty much the same speed, everybody moves about the same pace and you really don't see that many people."

A few holes between Springbrook and Trego Flowage (450 acres) hold muskies and walleyes (a Rice Lake angler hauled a 12-pound walleye from beneath the Highway 53 bridge in the early 1980s). But the best warm water action is on the flowage and below.

"Trego Flowage is kind of a sleeper for muskies," says Jeff Breaker, of Trego Sporting Goods and a river fishing guide. You're most apt to see Breaker's canoe west of the flowage below the County K Bridge landing. Difficult access keeps this section lightly pressured. Plan on a winding, 15-mile, 10- to 12-hour fishing float to the first takeout at Whispering Pines, another four miles to the next at Howell Landing south of STH 77, and several more miles separating Howell and Namekagon Trail Bridge canoe launch northwest of STH. 77 ... then you run out of landings until Big Island on the Minnesota side of the St. Croix River.

"Early August and again in fall can be good times for both smallmouths and muskies," Breaker advises. "The muskies might be planted fish from the flowage, but I suspect some come up from the St. Croix River, and a few probably are naturals."

On several trips down the Namekagon, I've caught and see others land walleyes over 20 inches on floating jigs rigged with crawlers or leeches. We've also taken walleyes below rapids casting crankbaits for smallmouths. If you're a flyfisher, the lower Namekagon offers unimpeded shore-to-shore casting.

National Park Service-maintained campsite fire rings are good shore lunch sites. Other than good-weather holidays, you're likely to find them unoccupied during weekday

IF YOU GO

For up-to-date insect hatch and trout fishing conditions, as well as a good selection of fly fishing flies and tackle, and information about Namekagon guide services and lodging, contact Pastika's Sports at Hayward, (716) 634-4466.

The National Park Service maintains close to 100 campsites along the Namekagon, and for visitor information call or stop in at the service's National Wild and Scenic Riverway information center an STH 63 northeast of Trego an the Namekagon River, (715) 635-8346.

Also, contact Bob Kinderman's Quiet Sports Outfitters sea kayak-canoe rental/shuttle service at Trego at (715) 634-7047, and Namekagon River fishing guide Jeff Breaker of Trego Sporting Goods at (715) 634-2333.

As local midway dining along the river, try the Dinner Bell Restaurant at Trego for breakfast, and The Prime across STH 53 for supper.

Chapter 2

Wilderness Fishing In Wisconsin

by Roger Sabota
Northeast Field Editor

Picture yourself sitting in the boat as the sun begins to peek through the trees along the shoreline. You search the shoreline and as far as the eye can see, not a cabin or other building is visible. Areas of the shoreline appear as remote and wild as they were in the 1940s. As you search the shoreline a doe and her twin fawns step out of the thick cover to get an early morning drink. There are two groups of mallards dipping in the back bay and a pair of eagles soaring overhead. And best of all you and your partner are catching enough walleyes to keep any angler interested in fishing.

This introductory paragraph paints a mental picture of a body of water which most people feel only exists in a remote Canadian location. Such is not the fact — there is a sprawling flowage located about eight miles west of Hazelhurst called the Willow Flowage. The Willow Flowage is an impoundment of the Willow and Tomahawk rivers and remains a significant addition to the Wisconsin Valley Improvement Company's series of water control lakes. There are nearly

Photo courtesy Roger Sabota

Northeast Field Editor Roger Sabota at the helm of his guide boat on the Willow Flowage.

7,000 surface acres of water in the flowage with over 70 miles of rugged, forested shoreline. One publication uses the phrase that, "the silence is penetrating" in describing the Willow Flowage.

Five public access sites are scattered along the shores of the flowage which will accommodate fishing boats as well as vehicles and trailers. One landing which is easily accessible on the east shore is located just north of the dam at the Tomahawk River outlet. To locate this landing take Oneida County Highway Y from Highway 51 to Willow Dam Road. Proceed approximately 2.2 miles on this road to the landing road and launch facility. A concrete slab ramp and dirt parking area for 15 rigs is available. This landing also has toilet facilities. Although low water levels may cause this landing to be shallow it is the best landing on the east side of the flowage.

Water levels on the flowage are maintained by a dam control structure which is 18 feet high located on the Tomahawk River outlet. There is an annual water drawdown of 15 to 18 feet which frequently begins in May. This annual drawdown has no detrimental effect on walleye population. The flowage has a vast and complex combination of structures which allow anglers to have countless days of exploration to locate their own "honey holes."

Several of the old time Willow Flowage guides will tell anyone who asks that fishing on the flowage today "just isn't what it used to be." They look at the sky and recall days from years past when everyone in their boats caught large numbers of walleyes including several in the eight- to 10-pound range. Of course comments of that sort will be made about any quality body of water in North America. Fishing pressure has simply increased during the past 15 years across the continent.

A Fishing Hot Spots publication describes the flowage as an area famous for the large number of bald eagles and its wilderness aesthetics. That publication cited the walleye as the dominant predator fish in control. The Willow Flowage has been described by numerous DNR fisheries biologists as an excellent walleye factory with excellent natural reproduction. Guides describe it as a numbers lake.

When the locals talk about the Willow they talk about icefishing as frequently as they do about open water fishing. Each winter the Willow is a favorite spot for those who enjoy watching tip-ups. Most of the discussions about fishing on the big flowage concentrate on walleye fishing, but frequently talk about northerns and big crappies will creep in. The Willow

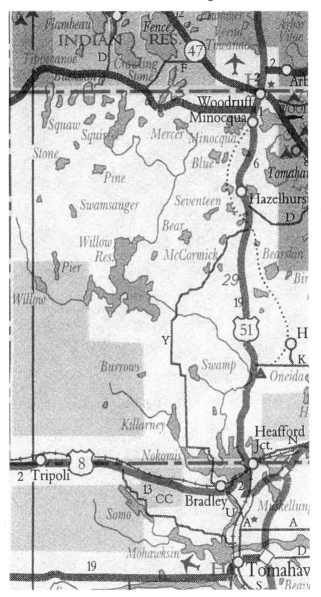

produces some excellent crappie action each year for those who seek them out. And Hazelhurst taxidermist Gary Schenzel will almost whisper when he mentions the musky fishing on the flowage. The Willow Flowage is not regarded by most as class A musky water, but those like Gary who learn the flowage can show some very large fish as the rewards for their efforts.

The water in the Willow Flowage is stained to the color of a well brewed cup of tea. As a result of the colored water the walleyes are able to remain in relatively shallow water throughout most of the summer with the exception of the very warm water period. The entire Willow Flowage is open for motor trolling which is the method of choice for many anglers looking for active fish.

Rhinelander area guide Adam Weise smiles so hard when talking about the Willow that the hair on his upper lip literally jumps. Adam claims that he can catch walleyes at all times of the year from the many river channels. He prefers to move his boat along the channel edge in 10 to 15 feet of water with the electric motor while vertical jigging with a jig and minnow. Once he locates active walleyes he drops an anchor and works the school with two rods. One rod is equipped with a jig and the other with a slip bobber. Adam also recommends that anyone who plans to fish the flowage should take a good supply of jigs along. He says, "She just seems to eat jigs."

Many experienced anglers who do well on the Willow spend a lot of their time in May, June and September working the wood. They have found that when stumps are located along the breaklines they tend to be walleye magnets. Weedless jigs or slip bobber rigs are very effective tools for catching walleyes from the many stumps and wood piles.

IF YOU GO

If you are planning a first trip to the Willow Flowage you may be well advised to seek out a good quality lake map. The many rock bars and stump fields are hazards to navigate for the inexperienced boater. Fishing Hot Spots produces an excellent map of the flowage. While fishing the Willow you may encounter The Wilderness Queen, a dinner cruise boat which takes daily cruises on the sprawling flowage.

For current information regarding fishing conditions on the Willow you may want to phone: Rollie and Helen's Musky Shop in Hazelhurst at (715) 356-6011 or the Island Sport Center in Minocqua at (715) 356-4797.

Chapter 3

The Black River Odyssey

by Tom Muench
West Central Field Editor

It beckons every summer, like the Lorelei of ancient times calling sailors to her watery bosom, when the July temperatures reach up into the 90s and its hidden holes and tree-shrouded waters give promise of respite from the trials and tribulations of everyday life. This hauntingly beautiful place which nestles ever so gently in the memory troves of the mind, is the Black River, with its secluded backwater sloughs and log-strewn holes and miles of people-free water and most of all, the smorgasbord of fishing opportunities it offers.

From trophy-class muskies to brawny flathead and channel cats, along with tackle-busting smallmouth bass and wallhanger walleyes, with crappies, mooneyes and alligator gars and an occasional leatherback turtle, the Black River from the dam at Black River Falls in Jackson County down to Hunters Bridge at US 53 near Galesville offers some of most exciting fishing and breathtaking scenery that you will find anywhere.

Photo by Steve Heiting

Feisty smallmouth bass are a major draw for fishermen to the Black River, says West Central Field Editor Tom Muench.

This river can provide a couple of hours of fishing respite or a day or a week or even a full summer, depending on your particular desires. There are several parks, island hideaways and endless holes and secret spots that even a summer is not enough time if one was to seriously fish every spot.

Perry Creek Park is one of the first spots you reach after leaving Black River Falls, located in the Black River State Forest just before the airport, west of STH 27. Hawk Island is just downriver from the park and is featured as a canoe camping area. This is about a four-mile trip from the rocks below the Black River Falls Dam and can be bank fished, as well as from a canoe. Walleyes, muskies and smallmouth bass are the main attraction in this stretch of the river. Muskies in excess of 20 pounds and big walleyes, with a 15-pound-plus fish taken several years ago, can be had in this part of the river. Deep holes below the boulders strewn throughout the river and the fallen timber and brush and log jams provide ideal lurking places for the predatory musky.

Moving on down the river, Hoffman Park, located on the west side of the river near Irving and seven miles from Hawk Island, is another full day's fishing trip, for there is plenty of structure to be worked, with an added bonus in the area being the chance to pick up a trout or two as Trout Run Creek feeds into the river near Irving and the wayside park. There is a canoe take-out and launch site at Hoffman Park.

The next stretch of river between landings is probably at least a two-day trip if you are going to fish it thoroughly, for it is about 10 miles to Melrose. In addition, there are some side-trips which are very productive in this section of the Black, with a couple of small shallow lakes holding some northerns, largemouth bass and panfish. Horseshoe Lake can be

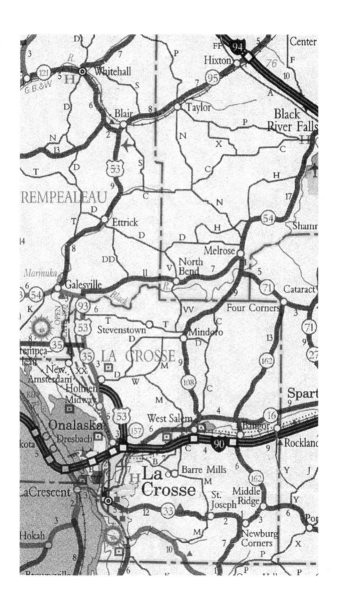

accessed from either Sunnyvale Road or Horseshoe Road off STH 54 which runs along the northwest side of the river.

My favorite trip on the Black is in this general area. It is an all-day affair which involves putting in at a primitive launch site about two miles east of Melrose, off River Road. You then paddle upstream for about a block and then take a cutoff run of water which is to the right off the main river. This branch wanders through some very picturesque territory and goes around a large island, eventually bringing you back to the main channel to the east of the STH 71 bridge south of Melrose. For this trip, you definitely need a canoe, for anything else will be too large to navigate the timber strewn structure you will encounter. You can also make this an overnight trip, for there are several spots where you can camp on sandbars, being alert to any weather conditions which might cause the river to rise.

The main attraction of this particular trip is the excellent catfishing to be found in the many deep holes. To be most successful, you have to work just about every hole and piece of structure, for the channel and flatheads are likely to be in just about any one of them. In addition, many of the same holes hold walleyes and if you are fishing alone, it is best to have two rigs or even three for that matter, with one set for catfish, one for walleyes and the third for muskies. If two people fish, one can be working for the cats while the other fishes for the other species. Either way, what works best is to tie up at the head of each hole or piece of structure and fish downstream into it.

Generally you will find the best holes at the sweeping bends in the river where fallen timber has created pockets of deep water as well as cover and natural funnels where food is washed down to fish waiting along or at the end of the current. Next are the holes formed below log and brush jams and the undercuts along the banks. The flat runs between big logs or trees out into the river can be especially productive. One of the biggest fish I have tangled with in this area was feeding in one of these runs and when I dappled a big deer hair frog into the head of the run, the huge maw of a musky blasted the frog and dove down into the structure, taking my frog and most of a 10-pound test mono leader with him, leaving a limp flyline and a lifetime memory.

Once you get around the end of the island, you will be back into the main channel of the river but will still have some considerable distance to go before you reach the take-out at the STH 71 landing. In this section of the river, you will find most of the productive holes along the right side of the river, although there are several spots where structure has been created in the main channel through debris pileups. The best advice is to not overlook any fishy looking spot, for the river structure is constantly changing due to high water conditions and changing currents.

From the STH 71 bridge to the take-out point at North Bend, it is about five river miles, with a broader expanse of river which allows the use of jon-boats and small fishing boats, in addition to canoes. There are fewer sloughs off the river but also more identifiable pieces of structure which should hold fish, with some real good musky holes in this stretch of the Black. There is also a real productive catfish hole just before you get to the landing at the Riverview Inn at North Bend.

From North Bend to Hunter's Bridge at US 53, it is about 15 miles, with lots of sloughs and a continuing widening river and if fished properly, would take several days to work. Even doing a fast trip will take the good part of a day, with an early morning start important. In addition to catfish, look for muskies, northerns and bass in this section of the river, along with good-sized crappies in some of the quiet waters.

Whatever your bent, whether it be for just a couple of hours or a day or a couple of days or longer, you will finding a fishing trip on the Black River a memorable event and one which will bring you back again and again.

IF YOU GO

As for getting about on a Black River trip, there are several canoe rental operations in the area where you can either use your own craft and simply arrange for being dropped off and picked up or where you can go the whole nine yards and rent everything you need.

The Riverview Inn at North Bend offers the following options — you rent its canoe and haul it yourself and arrange your own launching and picking up; you use your own canoe and have Riverview personnel drop off and pick-up; or you get everything from Riverview including life jackets and paddles and the shuttle service. Weekdays hours are 6 a.m. to 10 p.m. Weekend pickups are 10 a.m. and 2 p.m. The length of the trips can be worked out. The cost for canoe, paddles, life jacket and shuttle is $25 per day. The Riverview Inn also serves food. For more information, contact them at Route 2, North Bend, WI 54642, or call (608) 488-5191.

Black River Canoe Rentals is located a half-mile west of the city on STH 54 and is open seven days a week. Trip packages range from one

Continued

day to a week and the $25 per day price includes the canoe, paddles, life jackets and shuttle service. There are also special group rates. For more information, write BRCR at Hwy. 54 West, Route 2, Black River Falls, WI 54615 or call (715) 284-5181.

For lodging, camping and shopping information, contact the Black River Falls Chamber of Commerce, (715) 284-4658 or write 336 N. Water Street, Black River Falls, WI 54615

For fishing equipment and information, contact Moe Hardware Hank, 33 Main Street, Black River Falls, WI 54615 or call (715) 284-4621.

For information on the fishing and water conditions, contact the DNR Headquarters, Fish Manager, Hwy. 54 East, Black River Falls, WI 54615, (715) 284-1432.

Chapter 4

Winnebago System

by Brian Lovett
Central Field Editor

Many of Wisconsin's sportsmen have likely been to the Winnebago System, and certainly all of them have heard about it.

The images are ever-present: a stringer of walleyes pulled from the Wolf River in April; anglers lining the shore while catching bucketsfull of white bass; a huge sturgeon hanging outside a lakeside tavern in February; or a fish basket loaded with saugers on a hot June evening.

The water itself is hard to miss. The major components of the system — 137,708-acre Lake Winnebago, 8,857-acre Lake Butte des Morts, 4,507-acre Lake Winneconne and 14,102-acre Lake Poygan — comprise about 17 percent of Wisconsin's total surface water. Throw in the upper Fox and Wolf rivers and you have a fishery that stretches for miles through several counties.

All of the Winnebago lakes are relatively shallow and generally have murky or stained water. The Upriver Lakes — Poygan, Butte des Morts and Winneconne — were once actually upriver marshes, and still feature some remnant emergent vegetation. Lake Winnebago itself features a little structure in the form

Photo courtesy Brian Lovett

Central Field Editor Brian Lovett (right) and friends with a nice catch of Lake Winnebago system walleyes.

of rock and gravel reefs along the west shore, but consists mainly of huge, expansive mud flats.

Walleyes are probably the most sought-after gamefish in the Winnebago System. After several consecutive years of poor hatches during the late 1980s, the system has experienced three excellent hatches and one good hatch from 1990 through 1993. As of this writing, the 1994 year class hadn't yet been assessed.

Ron Bruch, area fisheries supervisor for the DNR, said the mid-1990s will likely see good populations of older fish in the 6- to 10-pound range, along with increasing numbers of fish 15 inches or longer.

"That number (of legal fish) will be growing each year for probably the rest of this decade," he said. "It's looking really good for walleyes."

Winnebago System fish grow at a good clip since there are usually good numbers of emerald shiners, troutperch and, as of the summer of 1993, gizzard shad to provide forage.

Fishing tactics for Winnebago System walleyes vary. The Fox and Wolf river systems are famous for their spring runs, when walleyes work their way up to spawn in upriver marshes. Anglers generally fish deep holes with shiners on jigs or three-way "Wolf River Rigs" when fish are moving up to spawn. Later, they drift and jig, set out shoreline cane poles with Rapalas or use other methods as fish come back down the rivers.

As spring wears on, action on the Upriver Lakes picks up, as does the Fox River fishing in Oshkosh and shoreline and reef action on the west shore of Lake Winnebago. Anglers often choose to jig, troll crankbaits or cast to windswept shorelines at this time.

During the summer, many fishermen troll for walleyes on the Upriver Lakes or for suspended fish over Lake Winnebago's expansive mud flats. One preferred method is to troll long, thin crankbaits behind planer boards.

In winter, anglers use tip-ups, jigging Rapalas or Swedish Pimples through the ice for walleyes.

The system also features a good sauger population. Bruch said fish managers don't have a great deal of data on the fish, but sauger numbers remain relatively stable with little or no management attention.

Many sportsmen take time away from walleye fishing each February to participate in the unique Lake Winnebago sturgeon spearing season. The Win-

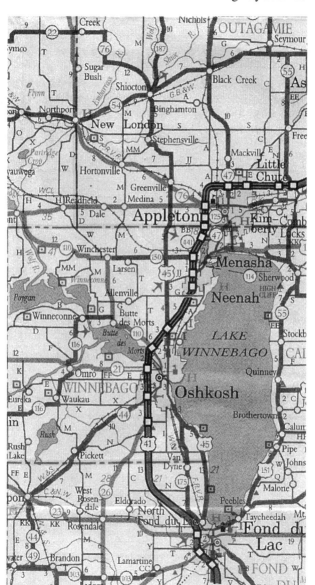

nebago System likely holds the largest self-sustaining lake sturgeon population in North America, and spearers are allowed to take one fish 45 inches or longer each season. A special Upriver Lakes season is held once every five years. Overall, lake sturgeon numbers in the system are good, Bruch said. However, there has been a statistically significant decline in female fish 68 inches or longer — those most desired by spearers — over the past 20 years. That trend has been documented in spearing harvest data and spring survey work.

For simply fun fishing, Winnebago System anglers can't beat white bass. The scrappy, prolific fish are currently very numerous in all system lakes, and there are also good numbers of older, larger fish.

White bass spawning runs up the Fox and Wolf rivers usually peak around early May and draw thousands of anglers from around the state and elsewhere. Towns such as Eureka, Winneconne, Fremont and New London become hotspots at this time of year.

During the summer, white bass can be caught almost anywhere. Look for schools of the fish feeding on the surface of the system's lakes. Small crankbaits or spinners will work well.

The Upriver Lakes support a pretty good northern pike fishery. Anglers often have good success icefishing in marshy areas or likely pre-spawn spots and good summertime action by casting to weedbeds or edges.

Pike numbers were depleted somewhat during the winter of 1992-93, when Upriver Lakes anglers experienced fantastic success through the ice, including numerous 20-pound-class fish. However, the 1993 spawn appears to have been very successful, and Bruch said Mother Nature is already taking care of the problem.

Yellow perch are a favorite target of Winnebago-land panfish anglers. However, a lack of vegetation near shorelines appears to be a limiting factor for the fish.

During the droughts of the late 1980s, low system water levels allowed for some regrowth of vegetation stands, which, in turn, apparently helped out perch numbers. In the past couple of years, however, perch hatches and perch fishing were poor.

Likewise, the Upriver Lakes and even some spots on Lake Winnebago can feature good largemouth bass fishing. However, the fish are limited by the amount of suitable habitat available.

Access to the system is excellent. There are numerous towns and cities near the system, and boat launch facilities are very good. Out-of-town anglers can usually find bait shops or taverns where they can get information about fishing, hotspots, weather and ice conditions.

One word of warning, however. The spring lakefly hatch, when millions of harmless but annoying flies rise from Lake Winnebago, occurs annually right around Mother's Day.

It may be the only drawback to what otherwise can be a fisherman's paradise.

IF YOU GO

The Winnebago System is massiv. There are numerous hotels, motels, campgrounds and resorts near the system. Anglers who visit the area can easily use the Yellow Pages to find restaurants, hospitals and bait shops around the region.

Here are the numbers of some chambers of commerce in major cities and towns near the system (area codes are 414):

Oshkosh, 424-7700
Omro, 685-6960
Winneconne, 582-4775
Fond du Lac, 921-9500
Fox Cities, Neenah, 722-7758
Fremont, 446-3838.

Here are the telephone numbers for some Winnebagland bait shops and resorts:

Jerry's Tavern, Oshkosh, 231-7380
Eureka Dam Campsite, Eureka, 685-5441
Wolf River House, Winneconne, 582-4555
Captain's Cove, Borth, 582-4757
Tuffy's Bait Shop, Fremont, 446-3799.

Chapter 5

Sturgeon Bay

by Dave Otto
Eastern Field Editor

The biggest problem with planning a fishing trip to Sturgeon Bay on Wisconsin's Door County peninsula is deciding where to begin.

Do you head out to the reefs for a meal of tasty perch? How about a deep water trolling trip on Lake Michigan? Maybe some fast smallmouth bass action in shallow water is more to your liking?

There's all that, and more, within easy distance of fishermen who decide to headquarter at Sturgeon Bay. And to top it off, you can stay at a comfortable resort or motel, or opt to pitch a tent at Potawatomi State Park.

No matter what month you come, some fishing will be hot at Sturgeon Bay.

In May and June, you can catch perch in Sawyer Harbor and along the shallow area known as The Flats. Then the perch action moves to deeper water. Try around the marker buoys along the ship channel, or take a run out to the series of rock humps known as Larson's Reef.

All perch don't go deep, however. Some excellent catches come from the weedbeds that line the deeper channel near the new highway bridge.

Photo courtesy Dave Otto

Sturgeon Bay yielded a brassy smallmouth bass to Eastern Field Editor Dave Otto.

Smallmouth bass have really come on strong in recent years, as evidenced by the popularity of the Sturgeon Bay Open Bass Tournament held each May.

The shallows of Sawyer harbor hold lots of bass, as do The Flats. Early in the season, work man-made structure like piers and breakwalls. Later in summer, work the deeper rock humps and the deep edges of the weedbeds for big smallies.

If you don't have a boat, then head for the stone quarry a few miles north of the city on the bay side. This is a first-rate shore fishing spot that produces smallmouth action right through the summer.

Walleye fishing, which was outstanding in the 1980s, has declined due to a series of poor year classes. Put there still are some trophies to be had, with fish in the 12- to 14-pound class taken. Work the rocky shoreline with jigs early in the season. Then shift to night trolling along the breaklines, or cast floating baits over the weeds in Sawyer Harbor.

After a 10-year lull, the DNR will start stocking walleyes again in 1994, so things look bright for the walleye fishing future at Sturgeon Bay.

Northern pike, long an ignored species, are now getting lots of attention at Sturgeon Bay. No wonder, with pike up to 29 1/2 pounds recorded in recent years.

Early in the season, try working the deeper edges of the ship channel with large jigs and minnows, Some of the best pike action comes in August and September. Cast big spinnerbaits around weedbeds and anchored sailboats right in town or near the new bridge. Another successful tactic is trolling large plugs along the Potawatomi Park shoreline for suspended pike.

Spend some time tossing rattling crankbaits around the edges of the large reef in front of the shipyards. A nice mixed bag of pike and smallies is always a possibility here.

Save time for trout and salmon.

In spring, troll for brown trout. Browns also work the park shore in summer when the water's cool

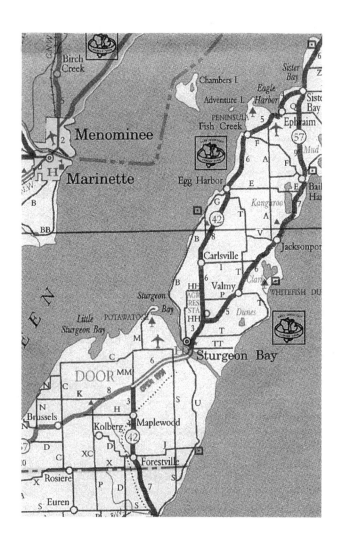

enough. Come September, the chinook salmon move into the ship canal and channel to spawn, and small boaters can get at big fish.

Otherwise, take your big boat — or hire one of the many charters working out of Sturgeon Bay — and head out into Lake Michigan for chinooks, rainbow trout and lake trout from May right through October. Just ask directions to the big reef known as The Bank.

The new fee launch at Sawyer Park right in town is an excellent spot to put your boat in. The ramp at Potawatomi Park has just been enlarged, and all you need to launch there is a park sticker. Sunset Park, another city fee ramp, offers quick access to The Flats.

IF YOU GO

Accommodations: There are numerous lodging and dining opportunities, but reservations are a good idea in the busy summer season. Call the Door County Chamber of Commerce at (800) 527-3529 and ask for a visitors guide. Camping is also available at Potawatomi State Park.

Fishing tackle and information: Mac's Sport Shop is the best place to stop, or call the fishing hotline at (414) 743-7046. It's updated daily. The folks at Mac's can also suggest a charter captain or a guide for some bass, pike or perch fishing.

Licenses: Resident and non-resident licenses and stamps are available at local sport and bait shops, and during the week at the DNR office adjacent to the Sawyer Park boat landing.

Medical services: Emergency medical care is available at the Sturgeon Bay Hospital, or by calling the fire department rescue squad.

Chapter 6

Lake Wisconsin

by Wendell Smith
Southwest Field Editor

Lake Wisconsin, behind the Wisconsin Power and Light dam at Prairie du Sac, is big water, covering about 9,000 acres with a maximum depth of more than 40 feet. It would be a good lake for a convention of Maytag repairmen, as they wouldn't get lonely. Lakeshore homes and resorts are plentiful and I-90-94 is nearby to bring anglers from a distance. The lake is very popular with recreational boaters as well as anglers, and with Wisconsin Dells, Devils Lake State Park and Baraboo such a short distance away, the area attracts a lot of tourists, some of whom fish as well as enjoy the other offerings of the area.

The lake is long, so the wind gets a good crack at it and can raise substantial waves for a small boat. However, a number of bays provide protection and are popular with fishermen with smaller craft and give families sheltered spots to anchor their pontoon boats or houseboats. A number of the bays contain fish cribs that attract panfish and bass and provide opportunities for shorefishing.

Grubers Grove Bay off Highway 78 just north of Prairie du Sac offers spawning bluegills in spring and

Photo courtesy Wendell Smith

Southwest Field Editor Wendell Smith likes to chase Lake Wisconsin bluegills with a fly rod.

has largemouth bass that hang out around docks, old timber and submerged vegetation.

Also off Highway 78 are Weigand's Bay and Moon Valley. A shallow rock bar at the entrance to Weigand's Bay is a popular spot for walleyes. Good baits there, and at other spots in the lake with rock and gravel bottoms, include chartreuse and glow-in-the-dark jigs tipped with a minnow and fished very slowly. Another good bait is a Lindy Rig with medium-sized minnows. Anglers should keep in mind that the minimum size limit on both walleyes and saugers is 15 inches. Deeper into the bay, fish cribs and weeds offer protection for bluegills and largemouth bass.

Moon Valley also has fish cribs to hold panfish and bass and offers some shorefishing opportunities. Walleyes can be taken by the bridge and in the stumps just out from the bay. Panfish can also be taken from the stumps.

On the south side of the lake, Whalen's Grade on County Trunk V is a popular fishing spot, offering considerable room for shore fishermen. A number of fish cribs are just off the grade that attract crappies and bluegills and especially in the spring good numbers of walleyes are taken. Behind the grade to the east is shallow Whalen's Bay. This water is well protected, a spot on the lake ideal for cartopper boats and canoes. A lot of weeds grow in the bay and fishing is best done early in the year before the growth takes over. However, for fishermen who like to fish the slop and work weeds with such things as a Moss Boss, largemouth bass and an occasional northern pike can be caught throughout the summer.

Also on the south side of the lake is Okee Bay, another partially protected spot with access from County Trunk V. It is shallow water that gets weedy

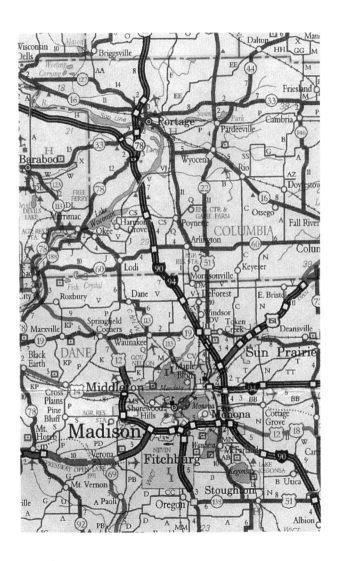

as the summer progresses. But for fishermen who know the secrets of fishing around the plentiful docks, it offers bass and panfish fishing opportunities throughout the warm months. Fishermen from shore and in boats catch bluegills, crappies and white bass as well as walleyes in the area around Okee Bridge.

Lake Wisconsin is big, with many more fishing areas along shorelines, in mid-lake, in stump beds, etc. and is probably best know for its walleyes followed by white bass, panfish and black bass. I have attempted here to point out a few spots where even the casual angler, who possesses a minimum of equipment, can wet a line and have a good chance to catch fish.

IF YOU GO

Maps of the lake are available at bait shops and are time-savers for persons new to the area. Zicks Bait Shop on Water Street in Prairie du Sac, (608) 643-6240, will answer questions and the Ace Hardware store in Sauk City, (608) 643-2433, can be a good source of information as can other bait shops and landings. The Lake Wisconsin Chamber of Commerce can be reached at (608) 592-3101. Adequate boat landings are available throughout the lake area.

Chapter 7

SE Root River Steelhead

by Gerry Johnson
Southeast Field Editor

In the past, when one thought of spring steelheading in Wisconsin, there was one traditional river that received and deserved all the praise. Fishing there was a springtime tradition that many anglers wouldn't miss. That river was the Bois Brule in northwest Wisconsin

Today, however, some things have changed. While still very beautiful, the Brule, and its source, Lake Superior, are not producing as many steelheads like they once did. Because of that situation, many of the Brule's traditional anglers are looking for a new stream — and some have found it quite a distance away. From northern Wisconsin, and from neighboring Minnesota, they're coming south to the Root River in southeastern Racine County

I get some satisfaction from that angler migration, and also from the many other anglers coming from Illinois and Michigan. I've been fishing the Root since steelheads began spawning in numbers here in the early 1960s. My spring steelheading ritual would begin on the Root and end in Door County, and it

Photo by Gerry Johnson

The Root River in Racine County has yielded thousands of big steelheads to stream anglers and is the best steelhead stream in Wisconsin, Southeast Field Editor Gerry Johnson feels.

included most of the streams in between. But even with these experiences, I knew my home stream, the Root, was as good, or better in some respects, than all these diverse streams I was fishing.

Even though its location is city bound, and next door to Wisconsin's biggest populations, the Root River is easily the best steelhead stream in the SE, as I have said many times in WOJ over the years.

Just look at its assets. It is connected to a proven fishing treasure, southern Lake Michigan, and more specifically, the lake area off the Racine coast which has offered some of the best fishing in the recent past. As a river, the Root is most scenic and beautiful with many gravel riffles for spawning, plenty of width for casting and wading, and numerous interesting holes, rapids and small waterfalls. In the spring it has excellent high oxygenated water stretches, and in the later years has become a "brood stream" where fish are netted for their spawn by the DNR.

This all adds up to a place where wading and shore anglers not only experience a prime run, but often take beautiful, silver-sided rainbows that range from four to 10 pounds, and very often bigger!

Bigger? Yes, Much Bigger! I hate to brag, but my pet river has been making news. On August 12, 1992, Murray Roberts, of Des Plaines, Ill., set a flyfishing world record on the Root. The steelhead he caught weighed 20 pounds 11 ounces, had a 37-inch length and a 20.5-inch girth. Most interesting, the fish had a DNR fin clip that identified the world record fish as one that was stocked in the Root in 1988, when it was only a few inches long

But besides trophy fish, what I like most about the Root as a steelhead stream is that it is consistently a challenge and a pleasure to fish. Even when steelheads are migrating in numbers, the fishing picture

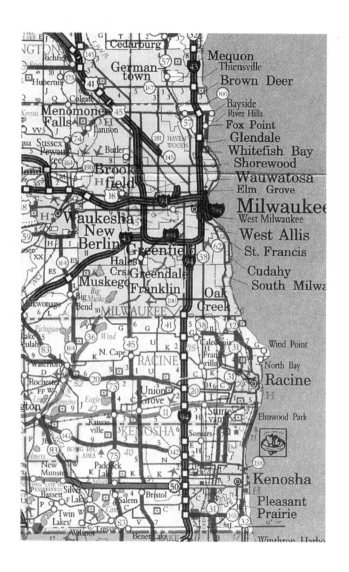

anywhere is never exactly rosy. The problem lies in the fact that all early steelhead specialists have normal spring river conditions to contend with, and an extremely cautious gamefish that is rarely easy to catch. Anglers should be ready for turbulent run-off, overflowing banks, finicky, finger-numbing weather, drifting ice floes, and simultaneous runs of suckers.

Not that you won't meet perfect conditions once in a while. On those days water is lower and more clear, riffles are playing sweet, sweet music, and steelheads are seen in the currents and on their redds (nests). Too, remember that the steelheads are primarily interested in propagation; they're not concentrating on steady nourishment while on their spawning journey.

Fishing techniques for steelhead vary with water conditions. In the wild water of early April, home-tied spawn sacks of fresh steelhead eggs are a top bait when drifted and bumped along the bottom. Drift them through the gravel and rock riffles where steelies prefer to spawn. Spawn for bait is usually obtained from fish caught earlier or kept frozen from the preceding season. Anglers without spawn can try the commercial varieties, but fresh steelhead spawn is a coveted commodity.

Later in the spring, when waters flow low and clear, more and more steelheaders are taking up the pleasure of flyfishing. Steelheads on the Root have been taken on brightly-patterned streamers, bucktails, and steelhead flies. The red or orange hues are favorites. The not-so-pure line of flies include orange balls of yarn or anything that imitates steelhead eggs.

But no matter what you try, you must drift your bait with the current, and be near, or bumping the bottom to get near the slightly suspended fish. In deeper water, are you snagging up frequently? Then you're doing it right.

By observing other steelhead enthusiasts, a novice can learn fast. Watch how the more experienced ones approach the holding areas and how they concentrate on riffles, fast channels, small waterfalls, and submerged limestone breaks.

Often they squeeze their spawn baits to freshen, or change them altogether. Hooks are sharpened frequently and leaders are checked for frays. Continually they silently watch for protruding backs, flashing silver flanks, and possible redds, and cast to all water commotions.

You'll notice also that the experienced fishermen will be dressed warmly and covered to mid-chest by quality waders usually of neoprene. Polarized glasses help reduce surface glare, and a big and strong landing net is available.

And unlike a lot of the steelhead rivers on our Wisconsin coastline, the Root offers excellent access to fishermen, and good fishing points in all these areas

There's the dam at Hwy. 38, Quarry Park, Colonial Park, and Lincoln and Island Park. All offer good water flow, spawning riffles and wading and shoreline fishing.

IF YOU GO

The Root River, up to its only dam at Hwy. 38 and County MM, is located entirely within the city of Racine.

Right next to the dam, popular with fishermen, is the Holiday Inn, (414) 637-9311. Other hotels visiting anglers have been using are Paul's Motel, (414) 886-2216 and Comfort Inn, (414) 886-6055

Racine Area Manufacturing and Commerce can give you more information, (414) 634-1931.

Campgrounds in the area are Cliffside Park, (414) 886-8450, and Sander's Park, (414) 554-8585

Racine has two hospitals, St. Luke's, (414) 636-2011, and St. Mary's, at (414) 636-4011.

Chapter 8

Upper Mississippi River

by Don L. Johnson
Editor At Large

It's the memories that keep me going back to the Mississippi River.

Recollections of boyhood days in the backwaters with a canepole and stringers full of bullheads. Years of memories of big bluegills, whopper walleyes and buster bass. Remembrances of northern pike rivaling any I've ever caught in Canada and Alaska. Flashbacks of good times with white bass, perch, catfish and even carp.

But the best part of going back to the big river is that there's always another memory in the making.

For sheer variety of angling, it would be hard to find more productive waters. Swift and slow, deep and shallow, they offer a real duke's mixture of fish. It's a rare time that you can't find something biting somewhere. The trick is to know not only the movements of fish, but also those of the river. It is dynamic, ever changing.

Reading the currents is basic. A practiced eye discerns the runs which fish are most apt to use and the eddies where they'll lie in wait of food. Divining

Photo courtesy Don Johnson

Editor At Large Don Johnson hefts an exceptional walleye taken from the Mississippi River.

what lies beneath the surface of quiet water is harder. Bottom contours may change dramatically, even in usually placid backwaters, whenever the river rages. However, while floods may wipe out favorite fishing holes, they also create others.

The stretches I love best lie upstream and down from the Alma dam, officially known as Pools 4 and 5, respectively. Between them they offer virtually everything to be found along the Upper Mississippi.

Above Alma there are wide expanses where, in summer, back channels meander through carpets of emergent vegetation, beckoning exploration. Encounters with panfish, largemouth bass and northern pike are most likely there.

Some four miles above Nelson, amid sprawling timbered bottomlands, the Mississippi is joined by the Chippewa River. A few miles farther up, the Mississippi widens into Lake Pepin. With such varied habitat, you're almost bound to find some kind of fish biting somewhere. There lies one of the secrets to fully enjoying angling on the big river. Don't focus on a single species.

Below Alma, much of the river has a wilderness aspect. Off the main channel there are meandering sloughs which embrace wooded islands and lead to quiet backwaters which you may have all to yourself. Birdlife abounds. Just the scenery and solitude are worth the trip. Most of the islands and bottomlands are part of a federal wildlife refuge.

The most popular fishing hole, though, is just below the Alma dam. There is a launching ramp nearby. However, you don't need a boat to try your luck there. A large fishing float, strategically anchored to provide varied fishing, is open for business daily from late March until November. A shuttle boat makes regular runs from a dock in town. The

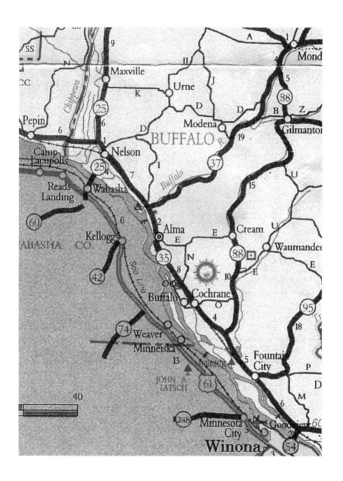

float has been there nearly 50 years. I can remember when it was hardly more than an oversized house-boat, but it has been much expanded and improved. Hot food, live bait and some tackle are available aboard.

Walleye and sauger action is usually best in early spring and late fall. I recall one late autumn day when an arctic wind was swooping down the river. I'd already had a good duck hunt near Alma that morning and decided to finish the day on the Alma float. Even my duck hunting gear wasn't enough to keep my teeth from chattering and fingers from growing numb, but the walleyes were hungry. Fat mallards and big walleyes. That was another day to remember.

Catches tend to be more varied in the warmer months. Panfish of all kinds, white bass, large-mouths, smallmouths, northerns and an array of other species. Catfish — both brute-sized flatheads and sleek channel cats — are most commonly caught in midsummer. Suckers, hackleback sturgeon, buffalo, garfish and eelpouts also occasionally come aboard. And if it's a fight you're looking for, don't sniff at a dogfish or sheepshead or carp. Mighty scrappers all, especially when they get into that current.

Anyone navigating the river also should know about submerged wingdams. Before the big naviga-tion dams were built in the 1930s, rock dams served to divert water from the sloughs back into the main channel. Riffles often reveal their locations, but don't count on it. If the water's up a bit, wingdams will be hidden, yet close enough to the surface to do violence to outboard motors.

However, a wingdam also creates a fine fishing hole, one you can count on year after year. If you can't find walleyes or lesser fry there, it may only be because a big northern pike is hanging around.

In sweltering weather, I've found big flathead cats lying below wingdams too. Newcomers to any stretch of the Upper Mississippi should be sure to stop at a local bait dealer or sports shop and ask about locations of such structures.

Getting local information is, in fact, the key to learning many things you should know. There isn't space to detail all of them here, and anyway, the rules, like the river bottom, are subject to change. Here, however, are some basics:

Do read all current regulations regarding fishing and boating on Wisconsin-Minnesota boundary waters. In general, seasons on most species are open the year around and bag and size limits have traditionally been more liberal than on inland waters. Wisconsin and Minnesota also have fishing license reciprocity on the river, but pay attention. There is an exception or two. Note too, that fishing regulations are not identical on both sides of the river.

Winter fishing is popular in the backwaters, especially for northerns and crappies, but beware: Currents flow through seemingly placid ponds and water fluctuations may further weaken the ice.

The Mississippi is federal water. Boaters should acquaint themselves with requirements for safety equipment and carefully review the rules of the road. Do not tie up to a channel buoy. Never dispute right-of-way with a towboat. And be warned that submerged stumps are plentiful in many of the backwaters.

Observe the limits when approaching the navigation dams from upstream or down, and familiarize yourself with procedures for going through the locks if you want to try that route sometime. Also remember that open expanses of the big river (and Lake Pepin in particular) can quickly become extremely rough if the wind rises.

Camping and picnicking are popular on the islands. There are many inviting sand beaches, so there is no reason for crowding.

And one other thing: Autumn fishing is often good in backwater areas, but if you find duck hunters already occupying a blind at a particular location, courtesy and common sense suggest that you should at least keep a discreet distance. Those guys probably were there before dawn, and their season is a lot shorter than yours.

To sum up, there's room for a variety of outdoor activities on the old river, and a boundless supply of good memories for all who come to explore and enjoy.

IF YOU GO

Alma is a picturesque old river town and the Buffalo County seat. Area accommodations range from motels and light housekeeping units to cabins and campgrounds. For a frequently updated fishing report, call (608) 685-3305. For detailed information on the float, call (608) 685-3782.

To access Pool 5, excellent public boat ramps and parking areas are located near the Dairyland power plant at the south end of Alma, and about seven miles downstream, north of Buffalo City on Hy. 00. There also is a ramp at 10th St. in Buffalo City. Camping and marine facilities are available at Great River Harbor, on a backwater three miles south of Alma. Canoes and fishing boats can be rented there, but no motors.

Continued

On Pool 4, a boat harbor and marina offers a full line of services near the north limits of Alma. Houseboats may be rented there, and cruises are popular on the 43 miles of river between the dams at Alma and Red Wing, Minn. For details call (608) 685-3333. There also is a public ramp just north of Alma along Hwy. 35, across the road from the Reick's Lake park and camping area.

Beef Slough Landing, on Hwy. 25 between Nelson, WI, and Wabasha, MN, provides access some 10 miles above Alma. There also is a marina at Wabasha. Lake Pepin explorers will find launch ramps and a small craft harbor at Pepin. There also is a harbor along the opposite shore at Lake City, MN.

Among good sources of local information are Rick Champeny at the Sports and Spirits Shop in Nelson and Jay Snopek at Backwater Baits in Nelson. The fishing is so varied that it's hard to recommend specific tackle. Below the dam, three-way river rigs are effective and jigs are popular. My top live bait choice for walleye is the willow cat — a tiny member of the catfish clan. However, they are usually hard to find. A long-time favorite artificial lure for working the tail-waters is the Sonar. For backwater bass, and northerns too, I often use noisy surface lures or shallow-running plugs with plenty of wobble. Snagless spoons dressed with pork rind are good choices in the weedier areas.

Chapter 9

Lake Mendota

by Tim Eisele
DNR/Legislative Update Columnist

Talk about a fertile fishery, good launching facilities and ample opportunity for family fishing, and you're talking about the Madison chain of lakes. Within the shadow of the State Capitol on Lake Mendota, the largest of the lakes, fishermen have an excellent fishery featuring walleyes and perch.

Lake Mendota has a surface area of 9,842 acres, with a maximum depth of 81 feet, and many bays and rocky outcroppings surrounded by deep water.

Lake Mendota is at the head of a chain of lakes also including Monona, Waubesa and Kegonsa, all connected by the Yahara River. The four lakes are rich in variety of fish species, but because of Lake Mendota's greater surface area, maximum depth, and shoreline diversity, it has more ecological niches and supports a greater diversity of fish species.

One important difference between the deeper Mendota and Monona and the shallower Waubesa and Kegonsa is the development of stable temperature stratification during the summer months. Species preferring cooler water during warmest months are better suited for the deeper lakes, where dissolved

Photo courtesy Tim Eisele

Gamefish populations, including walleyes, are exploding on the Madison Lakes. DNR/Legislative Update Columnist Tim Eisele shows off a dandy.

oxygen is occasionally mixed into the upper thermocline.

The result is that lakes Mendota and Monona are able to support large populations of more species of panfish at any one time, and Waubesa and Kegonsa, while having the same major species, often are dominated by fewer of these species at any one time.

Beginning in 1987, the Department of Natural Resources and University of Wisconsin-Limnology Center began an experiment in Lake Mendota to develop research tools to improve fishing and water quality.

The goal was to establish a better population of walleyes and northern pike, and with massive stocking of gamefish to test the theory that large predator fish will help improve water clarity.

From 1987 through 1989, Lake Mendota received stockings totalling 63.3 million walleye fry, 1.6 million walleye fingerlings, 30.6 million northern pike fry, and 48,600 northern pike fingerlings. In addition, the DNR began a year-round creel survey, intensive trap netting each spring, and electroshocking each spring and summer combined with U.W. sonar and netting surveys. Increases in minimum size limits of walleyes (to 18 inches) and northerns (to 32 inches) were also added.

Prior to the experiment, the gamefish population in Lake Mendota was less than one fish per acre. Today, the walleye population alone is 1.8 fish per acre and all gamefish combined number more than three fish per acre.

DNR Madison Lake biologist Mike Vogelsang says that, "Walleye populations are holding stable and we're seeing a nice increase in pike coming out of the lake, with many large fish being caught and released. Perch fishing is very good and should continue with recent excellent hatches."

A look at a typical fishing year, based on my experience and tips from Gene Dellinger, life-long Mendota fisherman and owner of the D&S Bait, Tackle

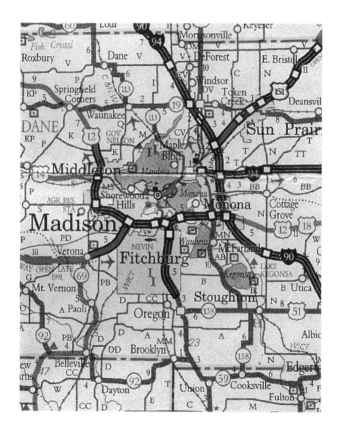

and Archery Shop at 1411 Northport Drive, Madison, starts with bluegill fishing immediately after ice-out followed by crappies.

"Crappies in spring start biting in the smaller bays where the water warms first, and then hit weedlines such as from Picnic Point down to the Edgewater Hotel and Second Point and in Warner Bay. About a week before Memorial Day weekend, when the water warms to about 64 degrees, you can catch crappies using a jig and minnow along the weedline," Dellinger said.

In early June, bluegills are in shallow water spawning, and good locations are off Fox Bluff, Warner Bay, Maple Bluff and University Bay.

When water warms to about 60 degrees, white bass will hit in Warner Bay and then out by Dunn's Bar and off Tenney Park. Spinners and trolled crankbaits work well.

By the end of June or early July, perch action heats up on Lake Mendota. A popular location to look for the perch fleet is off the "Four Doors," or boat house doors on the northwest side of the lake. Other favorite areas are Governor's Island, Maple Bluff, Tenney Park, Second Point and the old Hatchcover Restaurant on the west side of the lake. Hellgrammites are the best bait, but a Willy Worm or waxworm or spike work well on a small hook in 10 to 20 feet of water.

This is my favorite type of fishing on Lake Mendota, and it usually is going strong around July 4 or about the time of the Major League Baseball All Star Game. I like to fish just outside the weedlines and use spikes or hellgrammites on a 1/32-ounce jig. I put a 1/8-ounce pinch-on weight about a foot above the jig, and fish the jig just off the bottom, letting it hit bottom and then lifting it slightly.

Walleyes provide good fishing in July, with Dunn's Bar, Brearly Street bar, Second Point, the bar off the Commodore and Fox Bluff — all good locations. Use a jig and leech along the weedline in about 20 feet of water. Walleyes hit through fall, and some shore fishermen take trophy walleyes fishing the shorelines at night in October and November.

Lake Mendota has a good population of smallmouth bass, with some five- to six-pounders that look like little footballs. Beginning in late June, fish the bars and rocky areas off Maple Bluff, Second Point, University Bay, Edgewater Hotel, and the rock bar off Brearly Street.

Although some good-sized muskies are in Mendota, usually Lakes Wingra and Monona are considered better musky fishing in the Madison area. The lake also contains an improved population of northerns.

IF YOU GO

Lake Mendota is surrounded by excellent boat launching facilities, with Warner Park and Gov. Nelson State Park two of the best. Warner is a City Park where a $2 per day fee is charged, and Gov. Nelson requires a state park entrance fee.

Boats can be rented at Mazanet Marina, and bait, guides, licenses and lake information are available at D&S Bait, Tackle and Archery, 1411 Northport Drive, Madison, phone (608) 241-4225. Free maps of Lake Mendota, funded by the Madison Fishing Expo and showing facilities around the lake, are also available at D&S.

Boat Launching Areas: The Madison chain of lakes has plenty of excellent launching areas, maintained by the city, county and state. They include: Marshall Park, Warner Park, Tenney Park, Olin Park, Law Park, Olbrich Park, Goodland Park, Lake Farm Park, Babcock Park, Fish Camp Park, Governor Nelson State Park, Lake Kegonsa State Park.

State Park fees and city/county launch fees are required at these launching areas.

Chapter 10

Clam Lake
Fishing Haven

**by Steve Heiting
Editor**

As editor of Wisconsin Outdoor Journal, I fish all across our state, from the trout streams of the southwestern counties (after a hard morning of turkey hunting!) to Lac Vieux Desert on the Wisconsin-Michigan border for muskies, to Lake Michigan for the steelheads and chinook salmon it is famous for. I love to fish, but I also like to have something pretty to look at while I'm casting. And for that reason, I'm drawn back every year to the Clam Lake area.

Located near the junction of Ashland, Bayfield and Sawyer counties, the Clam Lake area is surrounded by the Chequamegon National Forest. It is some of the most remote country to be found in Wisconsin and is currently being eyed as a release site for an elk reintroduction program.

It's the combination of fishing and scenery that is most outstanding in this region, however. Everything can be caught, from panfish through muskies. Few — if any — cabins are found on many of these dark water lakes, and because of their smallish size and remoteness, power boating activity is almost nonex-

Photo by Kevin Schmidt

Though the Clam Lake area is best known for its musky fishing, nice walleyes can also be found there. This monster caught by Editor Steve Heiting measured 32 1/4 inches and weighed 10 pounds.

istent. And on two of the lakes — Lost Land and Teal — local ordinances ban speedboating, leaving the lakes free to fishermen and canoeists.

Here is a rundown of some of the larger lakes in this region:

• Lost Land Lake — At 1,304 acres, Lost Land is a fair-sized lake located about 12 miles southwest of Clam Lake. Its boat landing is located just off Upper A Road. With shallow depth and expansive weed-beds it's a fairly simple lake to fish and features muskies, walleyes, northern pike, both bass, crappies, perch and bluegills.

Lost Land is known more for the number of musk-ies it produces rather than size, but every now and then someone boats a 50-incher. Try casting a marabou-tailed Bootail spinner, a ShallowRaider crankbait, a Burt jerk bait or a Cherry Twist surface bait over the weeds for muskies.

• Teal Lake — Unless you launch at a resort, the only access to Teal Lake is via navigable channel from Lost Land. Its water is considerably darker than Lost Land's, however, and its structure is quite dif-ferent. While it has areas with plenty of weeds, Teal is studded with islands and bars and features areas of deep water.

Lots of muskies and walleyes are available but not in great sizes. Teal also is known for big crappies and some tremendous smallmouth bass. Weedlines are often a key on Teal, and it's wise to use brightly-col-ored baits because of the dark water. Deeper-running bucktails, like a French-bladed Bootail or a fluted-bladed Buchertail, and the DepthRaider crankbait and the Burt or weighted Suick jerk baits are best for muskies.

• Moose Lake — Actually a flowage, Moose Lake sprawls over 1,670 acres and features dark water.

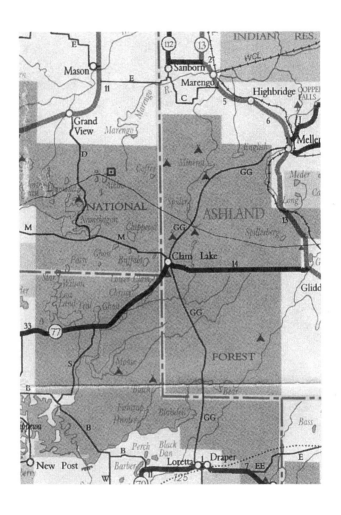

Three good landings are available, on the west, north and northeast parts of the lake. Fish species available include muskies, walleyes, smallmouth bass, crappies and perch.

The key to Moose, as with any flowage, is fishing the "wood" (submerged timber) or the old river channels. Jigs with brush guards are highly recommended, and the June walleye bite in extremely shallow water can be outstanding. Crappies can be caught on plain hooks with minnows, or on smaller-sized jigs tipped with plastic. For muskies, the key again is to fish shallow, so cast Colorado-bladed Bootails, ShallowRaiders, Burts and Eddies, or work the surface with a Cherry Twist, Hawg Wobbler or Tallywacker.

• Day Lake — Just a mile northwest of Clam Lake, Day is a flowage covering 625 acres that was created exclusively for recreation — it is completely surrounded by Chequamegon National Forest land. A campground, picnic ground and swimming beach are located on the east side. Built in the early 1970s, Day is a young flowage and change comes quickly to such waters. Muck bogs (local guides call them "ugly islands") pop up in late summer, though plenty of other boggy areas dot the entire flowage. Weedbeds are expanding, but because of the dark water they end in about six feet of water.

Muskies and crappies are the most popular species, with high numbers of each present. Fish near the bogs with minnows for crappies, especially toward evening. For muskies, twitch ShallowRaiders or Grandma baits, cast shallow-running bucktails, small Suicks and Eddies, or Cherry Twists and Tallywackers near or over the weeds and log jams.

Be advised that the lake has special management for largemouth bass — the daily bag limit is one fish, and the minimum size is 18 inches. Some big bass over 20 inches are present.

• Upper Clam Lake — Structure and nice weedbeds and plenty of fish — keys to good fishing anywhere, but seldom found in combination in a small lake. But Upper Clam Lake has it all, and with dark water it's a fairly easy lake to fish. Upper Clam covers 166 acres and is located immediately south of the village of Clam Lake.

Muskies, walleyes and crappies are available and grow to nice size. Weed edges are the key.

• English Lake — Twelve miles north of Clam Lake on County GG is English Lake, which is very similar to Upper Clam in that it has some structure, nice weeds and dark water. It's also a great lake to fish, with muskies, walleyes, crappies, perch and bass present in its 244 acres.

Use a Bootail, ShallowRaider or a small Cherry Twist over the shoreline weedbeds for muskies. Walleyes can be taken on small crankbaits in the weeds, or on live bait over scattered areas of hard bottom. Crappies suspend, but when you find them you should be able to put some hefty fish in the boat.

IF YOU GO

Live Bait, licenses, tackle — Renzelmann's Mobil in Clam Lake, (715) 794-2322, or Anglers All in Ashland (715) 682-5754.

Guide services — The Ashland Guides League can be reached through Anglers All, (715) 682-5754, or call Pete Maina, (715) 462-3952.

Accommodations — Cable Area Chamber of Commerce, (800) 533-7454, ext. 15

Medical services — Memorial Medical Center in Ashland, (715) 682-4563 (main number), or (715) 682-1153 (emergency).

Chapter 11

Embers of Washburn County

by Dave Carlson
Northwest Field Editor

Bob's brake lights, shining softly through a curtain of dust we'd been following for several up-and-down miles, signaled the road's cul-de-sac dead-end encircled by young aspen. Unloading on this sloping terrain, we simply opened the tilting vehicles' doors and guns, boots jackets, thermoses, shell boxes and three dogs tumbled out like an overstuffed closet. Scanning the tangled, hilly terrain, I again marveled at how Westerners label people from these parts "flatlanders.

As I laced my hunting boots, I reminded Bob, "A few years ago I ruptured an Achilles tendon and ...

"You young guys," the white-haired sage cut in. "What did you expect, a bicycle trail?"

Ruffed grouse were entering a cyclic period of decline, and southern Illinois friends Perry and Steve and I were anxious to sample what Bob told us would be some of the best cover this side of Heaven before the birds burned away like early morning fog over these tiny gems of little lakes in southeastern Washburn County.

Photo by Roger Sabota

Washburn County is a prime spot for hunting, ranging from ruffed grouse to waterfowl to white-tailed deer. Northwest Field Editor Dave Carlson bagged this snow goose on a hunt there.

Bob explains his plan: Steve and Perry hunt high over Steve's Lab. Bob is the center pivot with his Brittany. I and my springer beat the lowlands to do most of the brush-busting flushing.

"We want to give our guests the best shots, don't we?" Bob said, nodding as he threw his shotgun on his shoulder and waved us on with a "FORWARD MARCH" hand signal. Off we went.

Needless to say, Bob's plan worked to perfection. Actual number of flushes and shots and birds bagged over our five-hour hike truly escapes me. Pinned with medals of cut hands, bruised nose, and aching calves, I struggled uphill to my companions' afternoon sun silhouettes on a ridgetop skyline as they weighed the hunt's rewards ... a half-dozen grouse and several woodcock.

"Nice shooting guys, and now how far to the trucks?"

Bob points ... "Over that way, about a hundred yards."

"How'd we do that?" I said, recalling I never once saw Bob peek at a compass, although he'd obviously taken us in a long rollercoastering loop.

"You mean, how did — I — do that?" Bob says, his finger scratching his ear.

"Hail to the grouse-meister!"

A few minutes later, Bob's pickup disappears up the dusty road, and soon we're heading out, too. An aroma of leaves and brush on our clothes, freshly cleaned birds, sweaty dogs and last drops of coffee with chocolate cookies flavor conversation piecing together the hunt as forested little lakes and dirt-and-gravel roads turn to blacktop, and concrete highway.

And I see a grouse falling in a puff of feathers off a sandy road west of Minong in the mid-1960s, becoming the first "chunk" in this dreamy stack of Washburn County memories. There are flashes of more birds over the years, mostly the ones leapfrogging over the next hill or across a valley. And here come the whitetails vanishing into thick tamaracks and balsams, streaking through oak ridges, bursting across fire lanes, skirting tea-colored creeks and beaver ponds .

Bluebills rocket past my set of Cameron wooden decoys rocking in unison at the edge of a pothole-lake boat blind pelted by razory late-October snow. Ghost-like wisps of white — snowshoe hares — darting through logging treetops and tag alder clumps. Woodcock exploding in front of the dog's

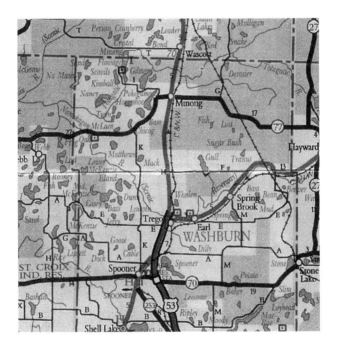

nose upward into the rising arc of a tradition-bent muzzleloader. Canada geese striking out in small groups from a picked cornfield covered with light snow as hunters hunker along a hedgerow. Ah yes, eating baked squirrel, iron-kettle three-bean beans and freshly-picked apples around a campfire crackling next to a still, glacial lake reflecting our camp-smoke in the midst of fall colors!

Some "cuts" on this memory woodpile show the youthful blunderings, slow and painful education, confidence-building discoveries and still-maturing appreciation for quality over quantity this hub of northwest Wisconsin recreation provides in its time, space and resources. A map of Washburn County and its lakes regions reminds me of two blasts at a target with a poorly-patterned shotgun. A smattering of tiny lakes are clumped in the southeast, larger waterbodies in the northwest. Large blocks of public lands surround or are close. While easily accessible by dirt and paved roads, much of the interior area is roadless. Throw in numerous named and unnamed creeks, several major rivers (Namekagon, Yellow, Totagatic), hundreds of lakes covering more than 31,000 acres and an ever-changing array of beaver ponds, and you've got a diversity hard to match in the Wisconsin northwoods.

"We've got something for everybody," says James Varro, administrator of Washburn County's 148,000-acre county forest, which covers about one-third of the county's land base.

Twelve scattered state properties account for another 4,732 acres of publicly-owned land. "A variety of timber types, and geologic activity ended and converged here," says Jim Pearson, of the DNR at Spooner.

National Park Service holdings ... owned and leased ... take in another 6,824 acres.

Varro says county lands are managed to allow "no," "limited" (under 700 pounds only), or "generally unrestricted" motor vehicle access. He points to the Birchwood Fire Lane area bordering Sawyer County where there are excellent chances of running into large-antlered deer. One such 16-point bruiser killed in the November 1993 hunt by Long Lake resident Tom Randall had a dressed weight of 265 pounds!

Non-motorized areas are relished by bowhunters who appreciate solitude and minimal competition, Varro says. Another prime choice for secluded big country would be Cedar Creek Recreation Area, three miles off Highway 77 in northeastern Washburn County. A quiet non-motorized favorite of grouse hunters is Welsh Lake Unit south of Shell Lake, an aspen-red oak studded watershed complex of ponds and lakes and intermittent streams. Management partnerships with logging interests, the Ruffed Grouse Society and DNR produce a potential 20 miles of hunter walking trails.

If there is any dilemma to the little lakes public hunting lands of Washburn County, it would be this: Can you risk leaving fishing tackle at home just because it's hunting season. I'd suggest definitely not!

IF YOU GO

An "Outdoorsman's Guide" to Washburn County (50 cents plus $1 postage), and county lands road-use maps are available by contacting Jim Varro, Forest Administrator, 342 Walnut Street, Spooner, WI 54702, telephone (715) 635-2886. Lodging and restaurant information for the entire county is available free from Wisconsin Indian Country, Chetek, WI 54728, telephone (800) 472-6654.

Chapter 12

Late Season Big Water Ducks

by Roger Sabota
Northeast Field Editor

It was a beautiful late October day to be sitting in a duck blind on a northern Wisconsin lake. The wind was howling at over 20 miles per hour, the temperature had dropped 15 degrees in the past two hours, it was alternately snowing or raining and the sky was full of bluebills. As we hunkered down to take advantage of the wind-breaking abilities of our blind we could see over 100 decoys bobbing in the waves. The decoys on the outer edge of the spread were icing just a bit but not enough to cause a problem.

My partners for this memorable hunt were a former college roommate by the name of Clyde, who has become like an adopted brother, and a spoiled little golden retriever by the name of Brandy who thinks she is human. Brandy was curled up by our feet on two boat cushions and covered with a rain poncho. She would snooze until she could hear the rush of air through duck's wings, then she was all business.

We were set up off the southern end of Cow Island on Lac Vieux Desert which is located on the Wisconsin-Michigan border just a few miles east of the Wis-

Photo by Roger Sabota

Northeast Field Editor Roger Sabota's son, Craig, with the results of a day's hunt on Lac Vieux Desert.

consin community of Land O' Lakes. Lac Vieux Desert is the largest lake in Vilas County with nearly 2,900 acres of stained water. This lake is a shallow body of water which quickly whips to a froth when the wind blows. Two of the more popular duck hunting spots on the big lake are Duck Point and Duck Island, both of which are privately owned and regularly hunted by the owners.

Although these two popular duck hunting spots are not available to the general public there are adequate spots where duck hunters are able to hide near a spread of decoys. Normally when the 'bills are migrating through northern Wisconsin a good number of them will stop briefly on Lac Vieux Desert.

To access Lac Vieux Desert take State Highway 45 north from Eagle River to County Highway E, then turn east on E. Proceed east to West Shore Road and turn left. Proceed north on West Shore Road past Sunrise Lodge to the National Forest Campground entrance. A relatively shallow boat landing with a large blacktop parking lot is available at the campground.

For those hunters who may be intimidated by the big water of Lac Vieux Desert they may want to consider Palmer Lake west of Land O' Lakes. Palmer Lake is also located near the Wisconsin-Michigan State line and just west of the Cisco Chain of Lakes. Palmer is about 640 acres in size with several areas filled with wild rice beds.

Our best action for the big diving ducks has been late in the season on very windy days. It seems that when the wind blows hard the big 'bills are blown off the larger lakes and they flock to Palmer for the relatively calm areas. Most hunters set up off the reed filled islands or along the high weeds on the shorelines.

Palmer Lake is located 12 miles west of Land O' Lakes off County Highway B. Turn north on Palmer Lake Road for about two miles to a blacktop ramp and parking area. An advantage of hunting Palmer is the wilderness setting where it is located plus the fact

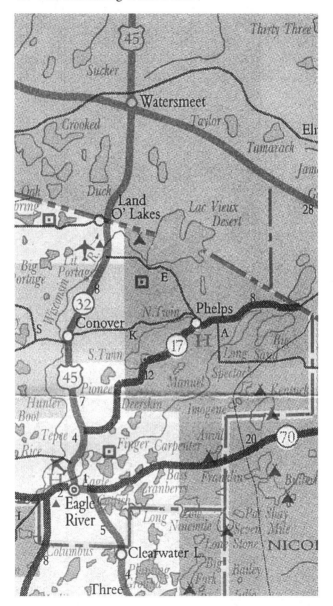

that hunters usually have the lake to themselves. With the numerous lakes in the immediate area there is normally a good population of ducks present. As previously mentioned a good blow will force the birds off the larger area lakes.

Back to the blind on Lac Vieux Desert on that frigid but magic day. Clyde was just filling our coffee cups when we saw a large flock of 'bills come low out of Misery Bay. They seemed to be looking for a spot to settle in. Clyde put the coffee jug down and went to work with his duck call. He is a master with the call and immediately got the attention of the large flock. As the birds got closer it was obvious that they were big birds just arriving from their summer nesting grounds. They were 50 strong and never circled our set but just pitched in. We both waited until the first few birds dropped their feet. After we put our guns down Brandy went to work and retrieved our birds. While she was bringing in our fourth bird Clyde dumped another which tried to join our fake ducks.

With only one more duck remaining for our legal limit we decided to wait for a large bird in just the right spot. I traded my Browning for a camera and we enjoyed a hot cup of coffee and a ham sandwich. Of course Brandy lifted her head from under the poncho to eat the last corner of our sandwiches, then laid her head on my booted feet. She has truly led a spoiled life.

Our final bird was the front bird in a huge flock. As they approached our setup with their wings set, the sound of air rushing through flight feathers was awesome. While Brandy was retrieving the final bird we lamented the shortness of the waterfowl season. This was the final day of the season and neither of us was eager to begin the task of picking up all those decoys.

A real advantage which many hunters experience is that these lakes are trophy musky waters. It is not unusual for hunters to leave the blind after the morning flight and trade the shotguns for a musky rod. Late fall is frequently regarded as trophy musky time and Lac Vieux Desert and Palmer are perhaps as good of lakes as one might find.

IF YOU GO

For up to the minute information about the duck population in the Lac Vieux Desert area hunters may phone: Mitch at Mel's Trading Post in Rhinelander (715) 362-5800, Eagle Sports Center in Eagle River (715) 479-8804, Dave's Sport Shop in Land O' Lakes (715) 547-3443, or Northern Highland Sports in Boulder Junction (715) 385-2134.

Chapter 13

Wild West Geese

by Tom Muench
West Central Field Editor

As the first slivers of light slice across the October dawn, the faint clamor of wild goose music reaches the ears of the two hunters nestled in the piles of corn chaff strewn across a picked cornfield somewhere north of Tomah in Monroe County. Now the goose music increases in intensity as a wavering skein of big Canada honkers appears on the horizon. Soon they are responding excitedly to the honk, herrronks which are drifting skyward from amidst the stubble.

The excitement builds as the lead gander swings wide of the edge of the field, his neck craning from side to side as he looks over the breakfast table. Convinced that all is well by the soft feeding chuckles coming from the stubble group, the gander turns back into the wind and with wings cupped and legs dropped into a landing mode, comes into the spread, greeting calls emanating as he talks to the decoys feeding contentedly on waste corn. Suddenly the chaff piles explode and the sky is full of thrashing wings and raucous honking. Two from the flock fall to the thunder of the guns and another October goose hunt is over.

Photo by Steve Heiting

Goose hunting in western Wisconsin has a big fan in West Central Field Editor Tom Muench.

For this old honker hunter and partner Fritz Pon-
gratz, this scene, in one variation or another, is
repeated daily during the Exterior Zone season for
Canada geese in western Wisconsin. While the Horicon and Central goose zones in the eastern part of
Wisconsin attract most of the attention of the state's
goose hunters, some of the finest Canada goose hunting in the country can be found in western Wisconsin, in the Exterior and Mississippi River zones.

Whatever your desire in terms of hunting techniques, whether it be firing lines, decoy hunting over
water, field hunting over decoys, pass shooting or
jump shooting, you can have that hunt amidst ever-
growing populations of Canada geese spending all of
the fall and early winter in the western Wisconsin
counties of Jackson, Juneau, Monroe and La Crosse.

In addition to the type of hunt you choose, it can be
carried out on vast tracts of public land, both state
and federal and on big water, small flowages and rivers, backwater sloughs and on private land, with the
latter consisting of corn and soybean stubble fields,
alfalfa edges and cranberry flowages. From the
sprawling Petenwell Flowage to the Mississippi
River over on the state's western border, including
the Necedah Federal Wildlife Refuge, the Meadow
Valley Wildlife Area, the Black Duck Dike 17 Flowage and the Van Loon Wildlife Area, in addition to
the private agricultural lands, goose hunting opportunities abound and there is no better time to do it than
October.

Field hunting, at least in my somewhat biased opin-
ion, is by far the most exciting way to pursue wild
geese and is my favorite hunt, on an even par with
spring gobbler hunting, for the same elements for a
successful hunt are necessary. You must set up properly, picking a field that is being used and then locate

in the "working" portion of the field, taking into account the wind direction. You also need to use camouflage material which is common to the area you are hunting, such as the corn chaff, plowed field brown; soybean gray and alfalfa green and your calling has to be good enough to fool not one but as many as a hundred or so wary geese. Lastly, you must have the patience to be able to lay on the hard, cold ground for up to a couple of hours and to keep your movements to a minimum, especially in those last minutes when time seems to stand still as the wary geese circle and circle and decide whether to come to your spread or to move to another field.

For a successful field hunt, you need to either make a local contact who can scout for you and secure permission to hunt a working field, do your own scouting and make arrangements to hunt a field, or hire a guide. Local sport shops have limited knowledge as to where the birds are working and area chamber of commerce offices can generally only tell if there are geese in the area, so these latter sources should only be used as a last resort or as a part of a more involved plan. On the positive side of the coin, the goose migration into the western part of the state is early and by early to mid-October, the majority of the birds are here and will remain until everything freezes up, which sometimes does not happen until after Christmas.

Once you have a field secured, plan to be out and completely set up with your decoys in place and all of your cover ready before the first streaks of light etch across the eastern sky. On clear days, the birds will fly early, while on dark, dreary and stormy days, they will fly later and longer. If a major storm system moves in, they will stay out most of the day, making only one feeding flight. In addition, on clear days, there will normally be morning and evening feeding flights so if you don't fill your tag on a morning hunt, you can still score. For that afternoon hunt, you should be set up by mid-afternoon.

In field hunting, it is extremely important to pay attention to the waste grain left in the field and where the flock left the field, for you need to be set up where there is grain left and not where the birds were. In scouting, look for droppings, feathers and tracks and then, taking the wind into consideration, along with the existence of any natural barriers, such as tree lines, buildings, etc., set up so that you will be in range of the remaining food supply. Geese will often land in adjacent field strips and then walk into the stubblefield and graze amidst the stubble.

Another factor which has a major impact on field hunting is when the corn gets harvested. If there are weather complications during the planting and growing seasons, the resultant late harvest will definitely affect feeding patterns and cause the birds to use fields they haven't used before. They may not return to their old feeding fields.

In addition, if the corn and soybean harvests are running late and there aren't any stubblefields available during the early part of the season, look to hunting green fields. Over the past several years, due to wet springs and summers, harvesting of grain has been later than normal and the geese have taken to using alfalfa feeds more often.

Green fields can provide some excellent hunting opportunities, particularly if there is some good cover adjacent to them, such as weedy fencerows or standing corn. We have gotten into some real good action, using green camo netting to cover up right out in the alfalfa or along a fencerow which is on the flight path for the birds heading into a feeding area in

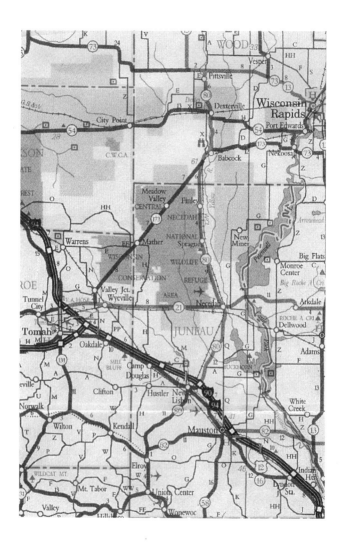

a field. Lay between the decoys and where the birds have been feeding, allowing them an area for landing where they will have to swing over you.

Another field situation you may encounter, especially if you come for a hunt later in the fall, is the plowed field scenario. As farmers get their fall plowing in, quite often the geese will be landing in the plowed area and then walking into a stubblefield to feed. We then use dark brown-black camo and set the decoys just into the edge of the stubble and then lay in the last furrow adjacent to the stubble, with that furrow usually being deep enough to allow our bodies to be below the ground line.

There is another situation which can occur at any time from mid-October on and that is autumn snows. This can create a field hunting bonanza, for it seems to increase the feeding flights as well as bringing down new birds fresh from the Arctic breeding grounds. It often presents some of the best hunting of the season. For these conditions, we use white camo made of sheets and again set up within good shooting distance of our spread of decoys, taking into consideration the wind and snow depth. Under snow conditions, we tend to use more decoys, mainly to give the impression that the field we are hunting is the place to be for any goose looking for a good meal.

In field hunting, there are a number of things to keep in mind and which, if carried out properly, will improve your odds for a successful hunt. First and foremost, be in a field which has been used by geese and still has feed available in it; secondly, always be aware of the wind direction when you set your decoys, making sure that the majority of them face into the wind and that you are in the best position to fire as the birds come into the wind — remember, geese usually land and take off into the wind; thirdly, keep your decoys free from snow and frost and make sure they have a non-glare finish; lastly, be patient, for if you are in a field which has been used, stick it out until at least 10 a.m. and even longer if it is stormy and the birds haven't flown yet. On far more occasions than I like to admit, we have pulled up stakes just a hair too soon, only to have honkers appear as we are pulling up the decoys or walking back to the truck. If you have the time, stick it out. In my hunting grounds, the geese are coming from large bodies of water and sometimes get up late. We must be prepared for them to come, for there is little in the way of feed on these roosting and resting waters and the geese will need to feed at some time during the day.

The Canada geese which provide most of the action in my part of western Wisconsin come from the Necedah National Wildlife Refuge, located north of STH 21, east of Necedah, in Juneau County; the Dike 17 State Wildlife Area located in Jackson County southeast of Black River Falls; and from several large cranberry flowages located east and northeast of Tomah, in Monroe County.

The Necedah flock works out of the Refuge in a number of directions, providing not only field hunting opportunities east over toward the Petenwell Flowage but also to the south of STH 21 and the railroad tracks and to the southeast toward Oakdale, Tomah and Camp Douglas. In addition, the outflights and in-flights provide some good pass shooting, firing line opportunities for those who enjoy that type of hunting.

The Dike 17 birds fly mostly south and west, toward agricultural land. Again, the flights provide pass and firing line shooting, along with some over-the-water decoy hunting on part of the property.

There are over 3,700 acres of public land at Dike 17, with the non-refuge part providing some good goose hunting for those willing to work at it.

In recent years, the large cranberry flowages have actually provided roosting and loafing areas for more geese than the public refuges and this has been, in large part, the reason for the excellent field hunting opportunities found in this part of the state. In addition, while these flowages can't tolerate lots of hunting pressure, there is access to some of them by permission and in some cases, by some very arduous treks up navigable but very difficult streams, which in turn results in some excellent decoy hunting for the big birds as they use the flowages. As always, it is wise to get permission far in advance of the hunting season, whether it be on a cranberry flowage or an agricultural field and to be more than a once-a-year visitor. Remember that these folks are generally busy with their farming operations and don't get as much time to hunt or fish, so a gift of game or fish or some other recognition of their generosity in sharing their land with you will be greatly appreciated by them.

At any rate, a western Wisconsin goose hunt is something which will stand out as an event you will always remember and look forward to coming back to, for it takes place amidst the beauty of God's Country, under quality conditions where you don't need track shoes to retrieve your bird and where ethical hunting is the rule rather than the exception. It's where the whistling of wild wings and the clarion call of the wild goose caresses your heart and makes it my favorite hunt.

IF YOU GO

Guide Service: Meadow Valley Sport Shop, STH 173 at 30th Avenue, (608) 374-2190.

Hunting Supplies and Goose Hunting Information: Meadow Valley Sport Shop; also R & E Sporting and Avon Shoppe, STH 21 & 173, (608) 372-3996.

Lodging and Related Information: Mauston Chamber of Commerce (608) 847-4142; Tomah Chamber of Commerce, P.O. Box 625, Tomah, WI 54660, (608) 372-2166; Sparta Area Chamber of Commerce, 101 S. Water Street, Sparta, WI 54656; Black River Falls Area Chamber of Commerce, 336 N. Water Street, Black River Falls, WI 54615, (715) 284-4658; Necedah Chamber of Commerce, P.O. Box 345, Necedah, WI 54646, (608) 565-2260.

Hunting Information, Rules and Regulations:
• Necedah National Wildlife Refuge, Star Rt. West, Box 38C, Necedah, WI 54646, (608) 565-2554; Sandhill Wildlife Management Area, Box 156, Babcock, WI 54413, (715) 884-2437.
• Meadow Valley, Wood County PHG, Juneau County Forest, write: DNR, Joe Haug, P.O. Box 1681, 2nd Avenue South, Wisconsin Rapids, WI 54494, (715) 423-5670; Area Game Manager, DNR, Black River Falls, Route 4, Box 18, Black River Falls, WI 54615, (715) 284-1431; Area Wildlife Manager, DNR La Crosse Office, 3550 Mormon Coulee Road, La Crosse, WI 54601, (608) 785-9000.

Chapter 14

White River Marsh Wildlife Area

by Brian Lovett
Central Field Editor

Steam rose off the river into the grey pre-dawn sky. Footsteps crunched through the frosty grass, finally stopping at the old ditch.

"Hear 'em honking?" one shadowy figure said to another. "They'll be flying pretty soon."

The Canada geese took their sweet time. More and more of them poured into the small oxbow, beckoned by the loud honking of their brethren. Sandhill cranes, content to lounge in a different corner of the marsh, piped in with their own brand of morning music.

Finally, the sun peeked over the pine-lined horizon. A thunderous roar of wings and water erupted from the river as flock after flock of geese slowly winged north toward their day's destination. One gun fired. Then another, and another. Three birds dropped from the sky as a hundred more flapped furiously to safety. An excited Labrador sprinted toward her first retrieve.

"Time for breakfast," I said. Our morning was complete. That was one scene played out a few years

Photo courtesy Brian Lovett

Pheasant hunting is extremely popular at the White River Marsh. Central Field Editor Brian Lovett admires a rooster he took there on a late season hunt.

ago at White River Marsh Wildlife Area. Waterfowl were the targets that October day, but the hunt could just as easily focused on deer, pheasants, small game or even upland gamebirds.

White River Marsh means different things to many people. The 10,908-acre state-owned property, located in Green Lake and Marquette counties, features a mixture of hunting opportunities and habitat.

The White River and Sucker Creek run through the property, and the Fox River marks the area's southeast boundary. The central part of the property is marsh, consisting mainly of cattails, sedges, reed canary grass and some wild rice. Brush marshes and lowland forests are also found around the property, and upland areas feature mature woodlots, grasslands and crop fields.

White-tailed deer hunting probably attracts the most attention at White River, according to Jerry Reetz, DNR wildlife technician at the agency's Berlin office.

Green Lake and Marquette counties feature some of the highest deer densities in the state. White River, like many public hunting grounds in areas that are heavily populated by whitetails, attracts quite a bit of hunting pressure, especially during Wisconsin's nine-day firearms season.

Nonetheless, the area still manages to produce some nice-sized bucks year after year.

"I think part of it is the big marsh," he said. "If some of those deer can sneak out there they can lay pretty tight and live a little longer. Some of that stuff is a lot of willow and alder and it's pretty tough to get at."

Pheasant hunting is also extremely popular at White River. In fact, hunting pressure during the opening day of pheasant season almost rivals that of the gun deer season opener.

"It attracts people," said Tom Hansen, former DNR wildlife manager at the agency's Berlin office. "There's competition for the birds."

The vast majority of pheasant hunting at White River is of the put-and-take variety. The property features very little natural reproduction of birds.

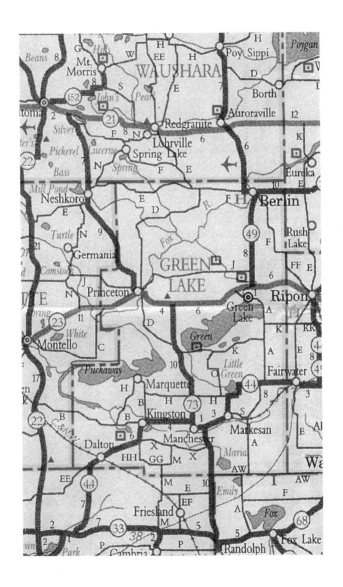

Grasslands on the property are heavily stocked with birds for three or four weeks into the season, and there is a 2 p.m. closure to pheasant hunting for the first two weeks of the hunt. Grass and cropland areas along County Trunk D, which runs through the north-central portion of the area, and South Road are the best places for hunters to check.

As its name might indicate, White River Marsh also offers many waterfowl hunting opportunities. The property features a lot of water, including natural marshes, rivers, streams and some small impoundments.

The property sees many forms of duck and goose hunting, but one of the most interesting and potentially productive methods is to float the area's rivers or creeks while attempting to jump-shoot puddle ducks.

"It's a great float, but it's a hit-or-miss thing, said Ron Koch, of Omro, who has floated the White River dozens of times. "One time I had my limit in the first half-mile. of course, I've floated that whole thing and never gotten a thing. I don't float to get ducks. I just like it to see wildlife."

Many people float the area with a partner, thereby allowing one hunter to paddle or steer while the other shoots. Koch said he prefers to make the trek himself, even though a White River float can involve several portages.

One partner Koch won't make the journey without is a well-trained dog, he said. Jump-shooting birds near thick cover or over river banks often means that sharp canine senses are required to retrieve ducks.

Koch said mallards and wood ducks are the main species available to hunters. Some teal are also present. The area sees almost no diving duck usage because there is very little open water habitat for the birds.

Reetz said there are usually geese available too, but their numbers vary because the area does not have a refuge.

Hunters who enjoy the simple pleasure of a day afield with a .22-caliber rifle — or the aroma of Brunswick stew bubbling in their kitchen — should also find White River to their liking. Mature oak and hickory stands around the property's uplands feature good populations of gray and fox squirrels.

The area's mixture of upland and wetland habitat, complete with thick willow and grass patches, also provides likely spots for rabbit hunters to check out.

There are also some grouse and woodcock hunting opportunities, but they are very limited.

Some pockets of the area also feature wild turkeys. However, there are not many birds on the public land. The area was once a turkey stocking site, but many of the birds have since moved five or six miles to the northwest.

If the deer aren't moving or the ducks aren't flying, White River Marsh Wildlife Area should still entertain wildlife lovers, Reetz said. The property is home to a variety of grassland birds, including bluebirds, meadowlarks and bobolinks, and is a major staging site for sandhill cranes.

IF YOU GO

White River Marsh Wildlife Area is located between Berlin and Princeton in Green Lake and Marquette counties. The area features dozens of off-road parking areas.

There are numerous resorts, guest houses, motels, campgrounds and sport shops in the Princeton and Berlin areas. Complete information can be obtained by contacting the Princeton Chamber of Commerce, (414) 295-3877 or the Berlin Chamber of Commerce, (414) 361-3636.

Both cities also feature emergency medical services: Princeton Family Medical Clinic and Berlin Memorial Hospital.

Chapter 15

Navarino Wildlife Area

by Dave Otto
Eastern Field Editor

If you were designing a prototype public wildlife area, you'd probably want a spot with plenty of room, within easy reach of population centers, featuring a variety of habitat and supporting a variety of game species that provide hunting opportunity throughout the different seasons.

The Navarino Wildlife Area in southern Shawano County fits this description nicely.

Navarino is less than an hour away from the Fox River Valley area, and only a couple of hours for hunters from the southern part of the state. With more than 14,000 acres in public ownership, there's plenty of elbow room, especially for those willing to work and get off the beaten path.

Hunters also find a nice mixture of habitat at Navarino. Much of the area is wooded, with hardwoods and aspen most common. Foresters oversee a regular cutting program on these acres, so there's always a good balance of succession between new and old growth.

Photo by Dave Otto

Shawano County's Navarino Wildlife Area yielded this mixed bag for Eastern Field Editor Dave Otto.

The project is laced with sand ridges that wander through wetland areas. There are half a dozen low areas with water control devices to provide good cover for waterfowl.

If you hate competing with road hunters, then Navarino is a good place for you. There are miles of trails, mostly along the many ridges, but almost all of these are gated and only walking is allowed. You can access these trails at a number of convenient parking lots on north-south access roads such as Lessor Navarino Road on the east boundary, McDonald Road which bisects the area and County Highway K near the Wolf River on the west side of the project.

Navarino gets heavy deer hunting pressure, both from bow and gun hunters, but the area still maintains a healthy whitetail population each year. There are some trophy bucks around. The secret is getting away from the easy trails and back in the thick cover where the big boys hide.

No matter what you hunt, hip boots are a good idea here. They will allow you to get to islands of isolated cover that most hunters avoid.

There's a lot of good ruffed grouse cover on Navarino, including aspen that was cut over five to 10 years ago. Grouse are down at this writing, but an upswing in the cycle could mean good bird hunting at Navarino in the latter half of the 1990s.

Woodcock hunters can have a ball here. There's a fair population of local nesters, but woodcock can get thick at the peak of the flight in mid-October. I know hunters who've shot limits and never got more than a hundred yards from their vehicle.

Waterfowl hunting is also popular at Navarino.

Controlled flowages near the Wolf River and along both sides of McDonald Road provide nesting cover in spring and loafing and feeding areas in fall, especially for mallards, wood ducks and teal.

A refuge area is posted each fall around the Pikes Peak Flowage at the southern end of Navarino, east of McDonald Road. This helps hold ducks and Can-

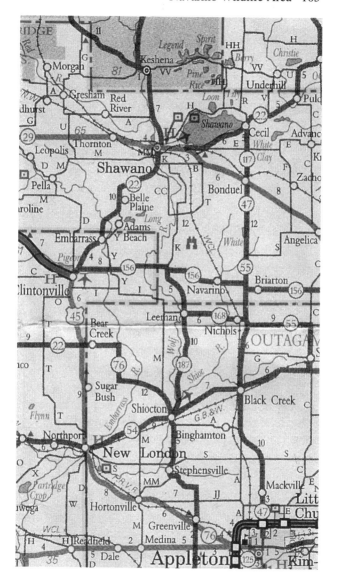

ada geese throughout the season, reducing the problem of burnout from opening weekend pressure.

Things can get crowded on the opener. After that, hunters willing to do a little swamp busting can find quiet potholes and flooded timber where they can set out a few decoys and do some serious calling.

Mallards and geese from the refuge have regular feeding flights to nearby farms. Do a little scouting, and you might get into some great cornfield shooting.

The real sleeper for hunters at Navarino is squirrels. There's an excellent bushytail population here, and it's lightly hunted. Work the red oaks on the ridges or stands of white oaks along some of the creek bottoms.

In addition to hunting, Navarino is a great place just to watch wildlife. Eagles nest here, and the project is home to a number of sandhill cranes. Check out the Navarino Nature Center at the southeast corner of the project.

IF YOU GO

How to get there: Take Highway 156 east from Highway 47-55 to the village of Navarino, and then any of the access roads into the wildlife area north from Highway 156.

Nearest service center: Shawano is about 10 miles north. There are a number of dining and lodging opportunities there.

Sport shops: Equipment and licenses are available at sport shops in Shawano or Bonduel, five miles northeast of Navarino on Highway 47-55. Licenses also are available during the week at the DNR office in Shawano (647 Lakeland Road).

Emergency care: Check Shawano Community Hospital, 209 Bartlette St. (715) 526-6464 for medical care. There are several veterinarians in the area. Check the Shawano yellow pages.

DNR: John Huff is the wildlife manager in charge of the Navarino Wildlife Area. His number is (715) 524-2183.

Maps of the wildlife area are available at the DNR office. Disabled hunters can check with Huff about using a handicapped-accessible waterfowl blind on McDonald Road.

Chapter 16

Lower Wisconsin State Riverway

by Wendell Smith
Southwest Field Editor

I sat on a rocky point, high above the Wisconsin, looking through a snow squall down the Wisconsin River.

Beyond my sight was the confluence of the Wisconsin and Mississippi rivers. In many ways, the valley probably doesn't look much different than it did in 1673 when Louis Joliet and Father Jacques Marquette, traveling with five companions, paddled their canoes down the river in search of "the big sea" and found the Mississippi near what is now Prairie du Chien.

It only takes a little imagination to bring to mind Jared Warner and three other pioneer families who came up the Wisconsin River and landed not far from the bluff where I perched. For them it was the end of a long journey. Those rugged people had poled and pulled their keel boats down the Ohio River, and up the Mississippi and Wisconsin rivers to start a new life and the community of Millville. The community grew until it was once a lumber and woolen mill boomtown. Now it is a peaceful Grant County hamlet

Photo courtesy Wendell Smith

Southwest Field Editor Wendell Smith and his American water spaniel, Buford, pause for one last look at the Lower Wisconsin Riverway after a day of duck hunting.

with a cemetery nearby where most of the occupants died of cholera.

Knowing a little history doesn't make the game bag any heavier with grouse or squirrels, and it doesn't lead you to a trophy buck or a long-bearded gobbler.

But somehow, it puts a little more romance and adventure into the hunt, thinking of folks who came to this piece of land on foot or boat or horse to seek game for the table. Thinking about such things makes the hunt more complete — better than just stepping out of the Ford Escort and walking away from the parking lot to look for game to take home to cook in the microwave.

Thoughts like these are what help make rivers my favorite hangouts. Lakes are nice. But rivers have been somewhere and are going someplace, just like the people who came before me, and those who will come after.

These feelings alone are enough to draw me to the Millville Unit of the Lower Wisconsin State Riverway in the fall. There are many spots overlooking the Wisconsin where I could get the same feelings. But here the land is public, so it seems at least a tiny piece of it belongs to me.

Much of the hunting land in the Lower Wisconsin State Riverway is marsh. But that is not the case with the Millville Unit. It is about 2,600 acres of upland and lowland hardwood woods. It is a popular place for squirrel, turkey and deer hunters. A few ducks are taken by jump shooters from inlets off the river, but it is not considered a duck hunting spot. Ruffed grouse also inhabit the property, but the last couple of years have not been good for southwestern Wisconsin grouse hunters. Birds often are hard to find.

Hillsides are steep and the bluff tops well above the river — tough enough going to ensure that if you are looking for ruffed grouse, you will work the birds slowly, and may have to shoot between the pants and the puffs. If you are going to hunt the hills, wear boots with traction. Slippery footing with wet leaves or frost is not uncommon.

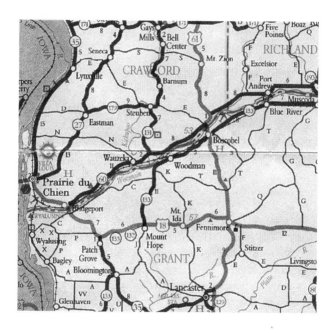

The Millville Unit is bordered by Grant County Trunk C. From the east, the site is reached by taking State Highway 133 from Boscobel, through Woodman and then C west to Millville. People approaching from the west should take U.S. 18 from Prairie du Chien, through Bridgeport, crossing the Wisconsin River, then east on C. Several parking lots are on the property. The Wisconsin River borders the property so it can be reached by boat or canoe with landings near Woodman upstream from the property and another landing downriver a short distance.

Overnight camping is not permitted on the Millville Unit as there are no water and sanitary facilities. Camping is available at Wyalusing State Park, 12 miles west on County Trunk C. Private campgrounds are located at Prairie du Chien and Bagley and a number of motels are available in the area.

All terrain vehicles, motorized trail bikes, snowmobiles and horses are prohibited and vehicular travel is restricted to gravel roads and designated parking areas. Operating vehicles off-road is not permitted. Hunters can use tree stands that do not damage trees and they must be removed each day at the close of hunting hours. If you are hunting the Millville Unit in the early days of the season, when the September sun shines warm, keep in mind that you or your dog could come across a timber rattlesnake.

As the Millville Unit is part of the Lower Wisconsin State Riverway, the regulation that prohibits possession of glass containers applies.

IF YOU GO

Questions about the property can be directed to the Wildlife Office, Wilson State Nursery, 5350 Hwy. 133 East, Boscobel, WI 53805, telephone (608) 375-4123 or Wyalusing State Park, 13342 Co. Hwy C, Bagley, WI 53801, telephone (608) 996-2261.

Chapter 17

Trophy Bucks in Southeast Wisconsin

by Gerry Johnson
Southeast Field Editor

Ironically, it has happened to a lot of hunters in the Southeast. It's November, and they have finally finished preparing for their deer hunting journey to the North. They leave early in the morning, planning to beat the traffic that buzzes around the SE urban areas. Often before they hit the I-System, sometimes less than five miles from their metro homes in the SE, a magical, SE trophy appears, a huge buck with a huge rack! It's not such an unusual experience. Besides such experiences happening to me several times, I know it has happened to several other SE hunters. That kind of experience ultimately makes you think, and the question that hits you directly is — What in-the-heck are you doing heading north?

Year by year, more hunters are realizing that the busy, very urban, and highly populated SE corner of Wisconsin is certainly not the place to drive away from during the deer season. It has proven itself, year after year, as a region where white-tailed bucks can grow big-beamed antlers in an amazing short amount of time. Big buck genes get passed on successfully

Southeast Field Editor Gerry Johnson approaches a downed buck.

every breeding season by one healthy buck after another.

So why do hunters tend to drive away from this area and head instead up north?

Well, first, it's not the lack of deer. The Southeastern deer story goes on and on with nothing but happy endings for most people who choose to take part in the action. There have been some population plateaus, but since that first deer season, the kill, for the most part, has been steadily rising.

Deer are even showing up in uninvited places — parking lots and driveways, backyards and subdivisions, and unwarily crossing busy highways. Areas surrounding Milwaukee, like River Hills, have been in utter controversy on how to trim down the great numbers of deer invading yards and gardens. Deer are simply expanding their populations and exceeding DNR goals, and the only real setback has been frequent car kills.

What we have are many whitetails scattered over 10 agricultural counties waiting to challenge hunters to some exciting farm and woodland action. Our land makeup is excellent, even though the traditional terrain that many deer hunters look for is mostly missing, i.e. heavy stands of pine, miles of aspen and scrub oak, endless stretches of hardwood ridges, and expanses of wilderness. Maybe it's that absence that looks unappealing to the crowds of hunters who pass it up to head North. But the truth is our SE land is growing more appealing to the local deer herd each year. Cover (farm-woodlot), food, and quiet refuge abounds, winters are merciful, and hunting pressure is minimal. The SE produces fast growing, large forked bucks, and in contrast, very few spike-antlered deer are ever seen. Most of the popular registration stations (Burlington, Eagle, Horicon, etc.) bring

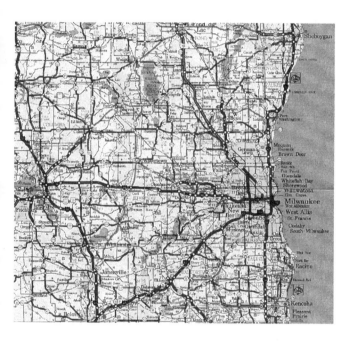

in about a half a dozen notable bucks each year from a hunter population that is not very large. These deer are minimum eight-pointers with spreads of at least 18 to 19 inches, with some spreads of 21 and more.

Most of my scouting has been done in Racine, Kenosha and Walworth, and I've really been impressed by the deer population in these counties. What's astounding is the quality of the bucks. I've stalked and photographed some of the "big boys," bucks with muscles bulging out of their shoulders, and carrying stunning racks. I've seen both typical and non-typical racks, and have seen groups of large, big-racked bucks running together.

During a recent spring season, I did some searching for shed whitetail antlers in Racine County. In four times out, I made three finds: two single antlers from different eight-point bucks, and then a tremendous find. I came across a matched set of antlers at the edge of a swamp near my home that, if all are counted, boasts a total of 22 typical points, all off of thick massive beams. A friend of mine soon topped that by finding a single antler with 14 points in the same area. Both have to be huge bucks, and I believe both are still around.

As far as hunting in the SE goes, I like the way wildlife manager Tom Smith summarized it when I talked to him a few years ago: "Hunting in the SE is a different mystique, a different regimen, a different atmosphere. But from a trophy standpoint, even though it's hard to measure, there's probably a higher proportion of large, trophy, healthy animals taken here in the south, than the north. And a large percentage of the animals are forked bucks — and they are big buggers."

Of course none of this is mysterious or secret. Many bow and shotgun hunters have known the potential here in the SE for some time. Many big bucks have been taken, like Mike Poeshel's Pope and Young 170 1/8 typical with 10 points and a 21 4/8-inch inside spread that was shot in Racine County in the 1989 bow season. But still, the exodus of hunters goes on. The same hunters who know the facts and the potential of the SE still choose to hunt in other areas.

We could list many reasons for the exodus. Tradition dictates somewhat where to hunt, and that is usually to the north, away from the SE. But a far more prevalent reason is the lack of open areas to hunt. Unfortunately, the SE is heavily private and visually posted to hunting, and in some areas there are firearm ordinances. To find a place to hunt you either have to know a landowner well, or be willing to work at getting permission.

Working at getting permission is not such a bad solution — but few do it, some thinking it is hopeless. First it involves research, finding where the big bucks live, then figuring a plan to get permission to hunt that particular land. This involves research and talking to people.

But to a few hunters, this type of thinking and investigating is well worth the time. The hunters who I know who have done it have become successful buck hunters with interesting tales of unique hunts. Some have given up most other outdoor activities, and instead, hunt and scout deer almost the year round.

So we definitely need to add some cleverness to our thinking. Certainly there are private places where landowners would consider allowing, if not a shotgun hunter, a bowhunter. Certainly there are croplands and orchards that are being damaged by deer. These are places you need to find. It's these private places where you want to go. I remember what SE game manager Mark Anderson told me some years ago ... "Some of the largest bucks come off lightly hunted private property."

So begin by talking to people about deer and deer problems in the SE. Let's keep our minds more focused on the deer of the SE, and our ears open. Then the hunting ideas will come.

Getting permission to hunt private lands in the SE could add new and exciting dimensions to your deer hunting experience. It could very well turn into deer hunting that is greater than anything you could have imagined.

IF YOU GO:

Southeast Wisconsin, as I cover it for Wisconsin Outdoor Journal, includes 10 counties: Dodge, Jefferson, Waukesha, Walworth, Washington, Rock, Racine, Kenosha, Ozaukee and Milwaukee.

Milwaukee is closed to firearm hunting, but some of its surrounding townships should be checked for their most recent regulations concerning bowhunting for deer. All other counties are open. Some of the best whitetail areas are nearby protected areas, meaning small towns and villages, subdivisions, country clubs, wildlife refuges, etc.

Other good spots border the well known wildlife areas, for instance the private areas in and around the Southern Kettle Moraine, Theresa, Horicon Marsh, Allenton and Jackson Marsh areas, Bong Wildlife Area, etc. For the complete SE area, camping and lodging accommodations would be too long to list, as would hospitals, but here are some telephone numbers of area chambers of commerce where you can get information on the surrounding areas.

Racine Area, (414) 634-1931; Janesville, (608) 757-3160 or (800) 48-PARKS; West Bend, (414) 338-2666; Kenosha, (414) 654-2165; Horicon, (414) 485-3200; and Watertown, (414) 261-6320.

Chapter 18

Meadow Valley Wildlife Area

by Don L. Johnson
Editor At Large

If we made a list of things that constitute an outstanding hunting area, I'm sure that most of us would rank two things at the top. First would be the availability of game. Second would be lots of room to roam while in pursuit of same.

Which is why I keep going back to the Meadow Valley Wildlife Area, at the heart of a huge expanse of public land in Juneau, Wood and Monroe counties.

Meadow Valley's 98 square miles includes wetland and upland habitats for a wide variety of wildlife. Moreover, it is bounded by many more miles of good game range, much of it open to the public. To the north is the 21,000-acre Wood County Wildlife Area, which is bounded in turn by the 9,500-acre Sandhill Wildlife Area. Collectively, those three properties add up to nearly 150 square miles — the largest block of state-managed wildlife lands in Wisconsin.

What's more, flanking Meadow Valley on the east is the Necedah National Wildlife Refuge, roughly 17 miles long and 6 miles wide, with various areas open to hunting at various times for waterfowl, small

Photo courtesy Don Johnson

The Meadow Valley Wildlife Area has been a productive ruffed grouse hunting spot for Editor At Large Don Johnson.

game, deer and turkeys. (In general, hunting dates on the refuge coincide with state regulations, but there are exceptions. The current federal rules should be carefully reviewed each year before hunting on the refuge.)

Truth to tell, the Meadow Valley area didn't make a favorable impression when I first viewed it. The land is flat, mostly, and the vistas seemed monotonous. I saw little that looked inviting in those wet meadows invaded by brush, the shallow flowages, and scruffy-looking woodlands. And the creeks? They'd all been turned into ditches.

But it didn't take long for me to change my mind. I soon discovered that Ma Nature, with some help from her friends, had done a good job of healing lands once badly wounded by axe, fire and dredge. Where proud pine forests had been turned into sorry farm fields, the trees had returned as aspen, scrub oak and jackpine (far more inviting to wildlife than was the virgin forest). Clearings bordered with hazel-brush and wetlands tangled with alders contributed to the diversity. Deer prospered. Grouse and woodcock thrived. Squirrels abounded. Waterfowl welcomed new, managed flowages. Sandhill cranes began a comeback. After some serious struggles, wild turkeys were established, too.

Small game hunting has always been the biggest attraction for me in the area. I like to poke along the ditches, following the brushy spoil banks and skirting around beaver flowages, tensed for the whirring flush of a grouse, the twittering rise of a woodcock or the splashing leap of mallards or wood ducks. There have been times when a hike has ended with some of each in the bag.

If you gun for grouse and shoot ducks on the same sortie, remember that you must carry only steel shot. In a 20 gauge with barrels bored modified and improved cylinder, I have found No. 6 steel to be reliable on grouse, woodcock and ducks jumped within 30 yards. Later in the season, when ducks are warier, I may switch to No. 4 steel. I'll also opt for the 3-inch shell if still carrying my 20. Adequately dense patterns for grouse are obtained with an ounce of steel No. 4s, but No. 6s are best while the wood-cock are around.

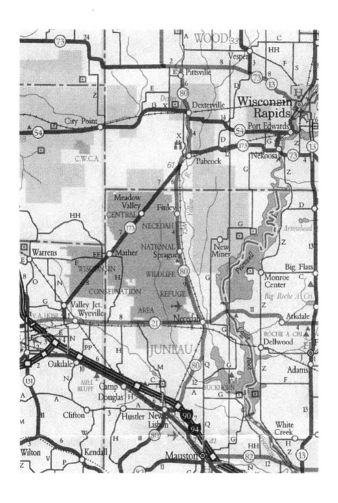

Waterproof footwear is recommended for traveling virtually anywhere in the area until freeze-up. Although you can usually find a log or a beaver dam for a ditch crossing, without suitable boots you'll find yourself taking frequent detours or getting wet feet. Also, carry a compass and a map. It's a big area, and I repeat, a lot of it looks the same.

For those wanting to try pass shooting or setting out decoys, much of the big Meadow Valley Flowage as well as some smaller flowages are open to hunting. Subject to special rules, waterfowl hunting is also permitted on the Sandhill area and parts of the federal refuge.

Limited numbers of daily permits are issued at the Sandhill headquarters, first-come, first-serve, for hunting waterfowl or small game.

Mallards predominate among the several species of ducks using the area. Canada geese are also present, but more are taken these days on nearby private lands. Squirrels are often abundant and are probably an underutilized game resource throughout the region. Cottontail rabbits and snowshoe hares offer further opportunities for mixed bags.

There are several primitive campsites in the Meadow Valley and Wood County areas, open for use from Sept. 1 through Dec. 31 without charge. I have fond memories of such camps, but if you use them early in the season, remember to take bug dope. Killing frosts often come early at Meadow Valley, but until then the mosquitoes can be fearsome.

The gun deer season is the one time when you might feel crowded in Meadow Valley (or anywhere in central Wisconsin, for that matter). The reason, of course, is a thriving herd of whitetails. However, trophy-size bucks are few, except inside the Sandhill enclosure where special management rules are in effect.

But in any season, the Meadow Valley country offers leg room for the hunter who likes to roam. The farther you go, and the closer you look, the better you like what you see.

IF YOU GO

Meadow Valley is located in central Wisconsin roughly 20 miles north of Mauston, 25 miles southwest of Wisconsin Rapids and 30 miles south of Marshfield. Highway 173, an old railroad right-of-way, cuts arrow-straight through the area as it runs northeast to Babcock.

The DNR headquarters for the Meadow Valley, Wood County and Sandhill Wildlife areas is located at Sandhill, about one mile west of Babcock on Highway X. More detailed information on those properties is available by writing Box 156, Babcock, WI 54413, or calling (715) 884-2437. For rules on hunting in the Necedah Refuge, write Necedah NWR, W7996 20th St. W., Necedah, WI 54646-7531, or call (608) 565-2531.

The unpaved roads which provide access to much of the area can be dusty one day and mires of soupy sand and mud the next, but should present no serious problems for the cautious driver.

For campers seeking more than "primitive" facilities, there are private campgrounds off the junction of highways 173 and 80 near Babcock. Motels and other amenities can be found within an hour's drive of anywhere you choose to hunt in the area. Many visiting hunters stay in Necedah, Mauston, Marshfield or Wisconsin Rapids.

Chapter 19

Grand River Wildlife Area

by Tim Eisele
DNR/Legislative Update Columnist

Grand River Wildlife Area is located in duck country, south central Wisconsin where some of the traditional waterfowl marshes have attracted migrating birds for decades.

This 7,000-acre state wildlife area, on the border of Green Lake and Marquette counties, was created in 1958, although local sportsmen saw its future as a wildlife area going back to the 1930s.

In those years the uplands and marsh were farmed and grazed. Portions of the marsh were ditched for farming, and those ditches remain today although a dam installed at the west end of the Grand River Wildlife Area now creates the flowage.

Jim Holzwart, Department of Natural Resources (DNR) wildlife manager for Green Lake and Marquette counties and Grand River property manager, said that the main emphasis for Grand River is as a waterfowl area.

"It is being managed as a deep marsh, with submergent aquatic vegetation plus the emergent vegetation in shallow areas around the periphery," Holzwart

Photo courtesy Tim Eisele

Though primarily known for its waterfowl hunting, turkey hunters have also found success at the Grand River Wildlife Area. DNR/Legislative Columnist Tim Eisele proudly shows a dandy tom.

said. "Upland nesting cover and grasslands are also emphasized."

It attracts a diverse variety of species, including diving ducks, puddle ducks (blue-winged teal, mallards and wood ducks nest there), geese (Giant Canada geese nest at Grand River) and non-game species such as Foresters terns, black terns, herons and cormorants.

The marsh holds northern pike and panfish, and the carp population has been held in check with eradication projects.

A chemical treatment in 1989 resulted in a drawdown, chemical treatment and restocking of gamefish. Fishing was closed until 1993, when it reopened, and besides helping the fishery the drawdown allowed plants to grow which attracted ducks.

The DNR has attempted to plant wild celery and wild rice for waterfowl, and is working with waterfowl groups to create additional wetland habitat on the east end of the property.

Peak duck usage of Grand River is about the second to third week in October, with goose numbers peaking the third week in October.

Mallards, ring-necked ducks, and canvasbacks are the major species to use Grand River, along with pintails, shovelers, teal, wood ducks, and wigeon. The variety of species available at Grand River is one of the things that draws me back to Grand River.

The Canada geese population usually numbers about 90,000 birds, with peak numbers up to 150,000 Canada geese at Grand River in the 1980s. The birds trade between Grand River, Green Lake and Lake Puckaway, going out to surrounding cornfields to feed. When Grand River freezes the birds move onto Green Lake, but will be back on Grand River if it reopens.

A handful of blue and snow geese are seen at Grand River, but not in major numbers.

Some hunters congregate near parking areas surrounding the Grand River Wildlife Area and pass shoot ducks and geese. Some skybust which causes crippling, especially near the observation point on the south side of the marsh.

Two boat accesses on the south side and one on the north allow hunters to take shallow-draft hunting boats out on the marsh and set out decoys. This involves some work, as motors are not allowed on the marsh and sometimes it is difficult to get through thick cattails to get to open water. Hunters may not park and launch their boat at Belle Fountain Creek.

The problem with Grand River is that because it does attract a good population of geese, it also attracts a good population of hunters and crowding can be a problem. On a typical opening day the DNR counted upward of 155 cars parked around the marsh. Opening day, weekends, and the opening day of pheasant season are days that I find the most crowded.

To avoid the crowding and find excellent waterfowl hunting, my favorite way to hunt the Grand River area is to hunt the cornfields surrounding the marsh. I drive around during the summer to ask permission of farmers and then set up my decoys in the fall.

The best arrangement is a cornfield with a pothole nearby, or a field containing sheet water after an early autumn rainfall. I use mallard decoys on potholes, and on land I like oversize Canada goose decoys which will not only attract honkers, but also mallards. Large flocks of mallards and skeins of geese will leave Grand River each morning and afternoon to feed in the cornfields or loaf on wetlands, and the hunting can be very good.

On the marsh be careful as you will see canvasback ducks, which in recent years have been protected, and tundra swans, which should not be confused with snow geese.

Grand River also provides pheasant and deer hunting, and spring turkey hunting. Beginning with the 1994 hunting season, the pheasant season closes at 2 p.m. to facilitate pheasant stocking and acclimation of birds to the area.

A refuge extends from north to south covering much of the open water on the west end of Grand River. With the opening of the deer season, the refuge portion of Grand River is open for deer hunting.

Canada goose hunters must possess a Horicon zone goose hunting permit to hunt Grand River and the surrounding fields to the north, east and south. The boundary of the Horicon Zone is Highway 22 to the west of Grand River, and west of the highway hunters only need the Exterior Zone Canada goose permit.

If Grand River gets too crowded, hunters have other nearby waterfowl areas including Mud Lake, Germania, White River and Lake Puckaway.

IF YOU GO

If you are looking for lodging, the nearest motels are located in Montello, about six miles north west of Grand River. The closest location is Stan's Puckaway Resort, on Lake Puckaway, which has cottages with kitchenettes, (414) 394-3292, and the Grand Valley Campground at the southeast corner of the marsh at the intersection of County Highways B and H (414) 394-3643.

To rent a private goose blind, contact the Oasis Tavern on County Highway B or Mr. Wally Walker in Kingston. Mr. Walker also has a special blind, built by the Wisconsin Waterfowlers Association, for use by handicapped hunters. The blind is handicapped accessible and is available at no cost.

Chapter 20

Wisconsin's Forest Crop Lands

by Steve Heiting
Editor

In the fall of 1984 I had just moved to northern Wisconsin and was in need of a new deer hunting location. Not knowing much about the area, I first obtained a county plat book (which gives the names of landowners), found three large chunks of property enrolled in Wisconsin's Forest Crop Law or contained within the Chequamegon National Forest, then purchased topographical maps of the areas. After spending a considerable amount of time studying the maps I walked the areas, looking for the best deer sign and best sites for a deer stand. The search took up nearly all of my free time for several weeks.

Finally, I decided to sit on the side of a hogsback and watch a ravine where several large scrapes and rubs indicated a big buck was using the area. On the first day I spotted three deer, including an eight-pointer that stayed in the brush and never offered a shot. That night I battled the flu until shortly before my alarm went off, but the memory of seeing the opening morning buck drew me afield.

Nearly 1.5 million acres of land enrolled in Wisconsin's Forest Crop Law and open to public hunting is spread throughout Wisconsin. Editor Steve Heiting has hunted this land for more than a decade and has taken some dandy bucks.

At about 9:10 on the second day I heard a deer trotting off the other side of the ravine toward me. I eased into shooting position and watched the trail where it cut through the bottom thicket. The next thing I saw was a huge set of antlers!

The buck had its head down and pivoted to follow the trail of a doe that had walked past my stand on opening morning. My first shot caused the buck's front legs to buckle, but it caught itself and leaped over a blown-down spruce. My second shot hit the running deer just an inch from the first and the 11-pointer was down for keeps. After a nine-hour, two-mile (according to the topographical map) drag on snowless ground, I finally got the whopper to my truck. He weighed 202 pounds at the registration station a short time later. I wouldn't mind getting another buck that big, but I pray that I'll have some snow to drag it on.

I've hunted that country ever since and have killed a deer practically every year. While scouting before deer season I have also killed a number of ruffed grouse, and while quietly stillhunting for deer during peak grouse years I've walked within short distance of more than 20 grouse in a day. I found a great place to hunt that fall, but what I did is something anyone can do.

Finding a place to hunt these days can be a frustrating experience. Fewer landowners allow visitors on their land to hunt, Wisconsin's national forest lands are located in the extreme northern end of the state, and state-owned public hunting grounds often get overcrowded. But with a little time spent in research, it's easy to find more than 1.5 million acres of land open to public hunting.

Where? On land enrolled in the state's Forest Crop Law. Every county in the state has such land, and it

Photo by Dick Larson

Forest crop lands in Wisconsin offer a wide variety of hunting opportunities, including many overlooked areas for white-tailed deer.

can be found either in county plat books or through a handy series of reference books called the Hunters Guide To Forest Crop Lands.

Wisconsin's Forest Crop Law offers a substantial tax break to landowners if they enroll their land in the program. Landowners pay as little as 10 cents per acre to a maximum of 80 cents per acre in real estate taxes if they keep the land wooded. For the tax break, however, the land is therefore considered open to public hunting, fishing, hiking, birdwatching and cross country skiing. No vehicular use or trapping is allowed without permission. Parcels enrolled in the program must remain there for a minimum of 25 years, with substantial penalties levied on those who choose to leave the program.

The program has proven extremely popular with lumber companies, which own thousands of acres of land. But large numbers of private landowners have enrolled as well. "And more land is going in constantly all the time," said Roger Benzschawel of Boyd, who publishes the Hunter's Guide series.

Most of the Forest Crop Lands are located north of Highway 64, but substantial holdings can be found throughout the state, Benzschawel said. Buffalo County, for example, which has long been known as perhaps the best trophy whitetail county in Wisconsin, has 14,000 acres of land enrolled as Forest Crop.

I've extensively hunted Forest Crop Lands for the past 15 years or so. I started deer hunting on private land, but lost that privilege due to the unthinking actions of another individual — the landowner closed off his land to everyone. One season of deer hunting on a public hunting ground taught me to look elsewhere, and a college buddy showed me some Forest Crop Law land in central Wisconsin. Having enjoyed that, I naturally looked at Forest Crop Land when I moved north.

Forest Crop Lands usually are far from the sterile, red pine-studded properties you might expect. Unless planted with a specific tree species, cutover lands typically regenerate with aspen, commonly called popple, and other sunshine-loving plants, which in turn yields great hunting for white-tailed deer and ruffed grouse. In many areas, the land may contain large numbers of oaks, which benefit all species, from deer to grouse to squirrels to wild turkeys. Just last fall a friend was bowhunting near a small pond surrounded by Forest Crop Lands and watched a flock of ducks settle in as darkness approached. He returned several times until the duck season closed and enjoyed great jumpshooting on mallards. Later in the season he arrowed a nice buck on the land, too.

Of course, land enrolled in F.C.L. may be covered with red pine and be undesirable as a hunting location. Therefore, it's best to cross-reference F.C.L. maps with topographical maps and drive the roads bordering the lands before spending time physically scouting the land.

Who knows? Forest Crop Lands may just yield the buck of your dreams.

IF YOU GO

Ten books are available through the Hunters Guide To Forest Crop Lands series, each containing maps for five to 11 counties. Each of the 10 books in the series contains more than 100 maps, and they also indicate all public hunting grounds and county-owned lands.

For more information, contact: Hunters Guide, Inc., 900 South County Trunk G, Boyd, WI 54726, telephone (715) 286-5519.

Your information Source for the Deer Hunting Market

DEER & DEER HUNTING:
A Hunter's Guide to Deer Behavior & Hunting Techniques
Al Hofacker, Editor

Get one of the finest whitetail hunting guides available. Al Hofacker, founder and former editor of DEER & DEER HUNTING gives you the best information ever published in DEER & DEER HUNTING, providing tips and insights into whitetail communication, activity, rubs, scrapes, the rut, hunting techniques and much more. Includes 100 large-size full-color photos of the whitetail in its natural habitat.

$34⁹⁵

8-1/2"x11 in, 208 pg. hardcover

DEER & DEER HUNTING
A Hunter's Guide to Deer Behavior and Hunting Techniques
Edited by Al Hofacker

Learn from the experts!

Order yours today from

Krause Publications
Book Dept. VOH1
700 E. State St.
Iola, WI 54990-0001

Satisfaction **GUARANTEED**

Include $2.50 shipping for the first book. WI residents add 5.5% sales tax.
Dept. VOH1

MasterCard or VISA customers call toll-free

800-258-0929

Books Make Lasting Gifts!